E
742
.A67

America's heritage in
the twentieth century

DATE DUE			

AMERICA'S HERITAGE

IN THE TWENTIETH CENTURY

Charles Bussey
John M. Carroll
William MacDonald
John W. Storey

FORUM PRESS

Published simultaneously in Canada

Printed in the United States of America

Library of Congress Catalog Card Number: 78:52125

ISBN: 0-83273-275-7

Cover Design by Cecil King

CONTENTS

To

Donna Bussey

Susannah Carroll

Janet C. MacDonald

Gail Storey

PREFACE

This book contains twelve original essays on the main themes of twentieth century American history. The authors, although dealing with sophisticated, scholarly material, have made an effort to write clearly and understandably for the undergraduate so that his reading in history will be both meaningful and enjoyable. Designed to complement a standard United States history text, this book presents interpretive material, new viewpoints as well as traditional ones, and can, therefore, assist in stimulating class discussion. It should serve to present American history as an exciting, thought-provoking study rather than a mere collection of facts.

AMERICA'S HERITAGE IN THE TWENTIETH CEN-TURY is divided into three interrelated parts with a general introduction. The general introduction emphasizes one of the important areas of historical study which is often overlooked in college survey courses. The word historiography often frightens or confounds students who find it difficult enough to absorb and understand one interpretation of the American past. And yet, the interpretation of history is often one of the most exciting and rewarding aspects of learning history. How can historians, using essentially the same facts, arrive at totally different versions of what comprises the American experience? The initial essay in the book attempts to answer this question by tracing the development of the various interpretations of twentieth century American history from the so-called Traditional view to the revisionist or New Left interpretation. The essay demonstrates that "dry as dust facts" are often the ammunition of serious historical combat in which scholars wage an eternal battle to uncover the meaning of the American heritage. Part one, the American Industry and Society Section, deals with the impact of American technology and industry on American life and covers such diverse topics as the impact of the automobile in shaping American values and attitudes; the emergence of American corporations and their influence not only on American history but on world history as well; the major intellectual and social changes that accompanied these industrial changes; and, finally, the impact of industrialization on American Southern life. Part two, the American Politics and Foreign Policy Section, analyzes the response of American politics toward economic industrialization, America's reaction to the two world wars of the twentieth century, the Cold War and its influence on American foreign affairs, and the emergence of the imperial presidency, a resulting development of the above factors. Part three, the American Quest for Equality and Justice Section, focuses on the various liberation movements in American history during the twentieth century, beginning with the black civil rights movements, continuing with the present minority social justice movements in the United States, and concluding with the impact that these movements have on the emotional makeup of Americans.

We would like to acknowledge a number of persons whose help was vital to the completion of this book. Many colleagues and friends read parts of this book in manuscript, offering both assistance and encouragement. In particular we would like to thank Professors L. H. Harrison, J. D. Harrington, J. W. Thacker, Jr., and Mary Ellen Miller, all of Western Kentucky University; Professor J. W. Harper of Texas Tech University, E. J. Hindman of Sul Ross University, and Professor Adrian Anderson of Lamar University. We wish to thank Ms. Jane Brown, Conney Shams, and especially Frances Shelton for preparing the essays for publication. We wish also to thank the various museums, picture agencies, archives and individuals who helped us locate and obtain illustrations. The authors also wish to express their appreciation to the staff of Forum Press, especially to Vandora Elfrink for her editorial guidance and to

Erby M. Young, Managing Director of Forum Press who initiated the project. Finally, we wish to express our sincere gratitude to the historians who contributed essays to this book. They were helpful, met deadlines, and accepted our editorial revisions with remarkable courtesy.

Charles Bussey
John M. Carroll
William W. MacDonald
John W. Storey

President John F. Kennedy is greeted by historian Arthur M. Schlesinger, Jr. (United Press International)

Reassessing America's Past

JOHN M. CARROLL

Few beginning college history students fully realize that the view of past events which they hear about in class or read about in their textbooks is constantly being revised and reinterpreted by historians. Usually there is not sufficient time in introductory courses to explore the three or four different interpretations which scholars have developed on a given event or historical movement. But the study of history is replete with numerous different views on the events of the past and their significance, and many of these interpretations are conflicting and contradictory. This may seem strange to students who firmly believe that what they hear in classroom lectures or read in their texts is the way it happened and why it happened. It is useful, therefore, to discuss the various interpretations of twentieth century American history to acquaint students with the multiple views of the past which are sometimes omitted in survey courses. It also might come as a surprise to beginning history students that most historians consider the study of historical interpretations (historiography) the most interesting and exciting part of their work.

The most recent comprehensive reinterpretation of American history from a unified perspective has been written by the so-called New Left historians during the past two decades. These scholars are called the New Left because they are the intellectual successors of an earlier group of historians, the Old

Left, who reinterpreted United States history during the early decades of the century by placing great emphasis on economic factors in the shaping of past events. Actually there have been four basic phases in the reinterpretation and rewriting of American history. It would be useful to briefly identify these four stages of revision and the major reassessments of the American past made in each period before returning to a more in-depth discussion of the New Left. The four major interpretations of United States history have been written from the Traditional, socioeconomic, consensus, and New Left viewpoints.

Prior to 1910, most books and articles dealing with American history were written from what today is called the Traditional perspective. These Traditionalist historians tended to be highly nationalistic and they wrote approvingly about American institutions and ideas. Traditionalists emphasized the importance of men and ideas in history and stressed the fact that the United States had a special mission in the world — to stand as a shining example of a republican society for the rest of the world to emulate. They viewed the American government and society as highly principled and dedicated to the fulfillment of the hopes and aspirations outlined in the Declaration of Independence. One of the early Traditionalists, George Bancroft, *A History of the United States* (1837-74), saw the hand of God guiding America in its struggle to maintain its free institutions and national independence in a hostile world. In general, Traditionalists praised the American system of government and viewed the nation's foreign policy as basically isolationist, but courageous in its effort to defend and inspire freedom and justice throughout the world.

During the early twentieth century and especially after World War I, historians emphasizing a socioeconomic view of the past criticized the Traditional approach to the study of United States history. These scholars, highly influenced by the ideas of Karl Marx and Sigmund Freud, believed that the Traditionalists placed too much importance on principles and ideas in history, and neglected the social and economic forces which shaped events. In their view, men were motivated not so much by abstract ideas, but by economic self-interest and by their irrational subconscious urges — concepts which had been stressed by Marx and Freud. The socioeconomic historians maintained that American history was primarily the story of the conflict and collision of social and economic forces within society. According to the socioeconomic or Progressive historians as they were sometimes called, men were the victims of social and economic movements which they did not fully understand and they simply used ideas and the rhetoric of abstract idealism to rationalize their behavior. Charles Beard in *An Economic Interpretation of the Constitution of the United States* (1913) maintained, for example, that the men who drafted the Constitution were not high-minded patriots as the Traditionalists had claimed, but men primarily concerned with protecting their material interests. Frederick J. Turner, one of the pioneer social historians, attacked the widely accepted view that the nation's accomplishments were wrought by great individual heroes and that they in turn were the product of a genius peculiar to the American people. In his "Frontier Thesis," Turner called for a detailed and critical examination of the effect of environment and social forces on American development.

The more extreme socioeconomic revisionists, the Marxists or Old Left, maintained that history was shaped and molded almost exclusively by economic forces. These writers, who were the intellectual predecessors of the New Left, were doctrinaire, and like Marx held that society was moving unalterably from a capitalist to a socialist era. In the 1930s, Old Left historians such as Louis Hacker and Herbert Aptheker emphasized the importance of economic factors in the unfolding of American history and indicted the ruling capitalist classes for oppressing and exploiting the workers and farmers. Clearly, the prominence enjoyed by the Old Left in the thirties reflected the despair and economic misery which intellectuals felt amidst the great economic collapse of the Great Depression.

After World War II, however, the mood and outlook of American historians changed dramatically. Most postwar scholars began to challenge the assumptions of the Progressive historians of the previous decades. If economic conflict was the key to history, they asked, then how did the United States survive a world depression and a massive world war with its values and institutions basically intact? In examining this question, a new generation of historians, including some who had previously held the socioeconomic view of American development, suggested that there was something unique and exceptional in the American experience. Postwar scholars such as Daniel Boorstin and Louis Hartz maintained that it was not conflict and class struggle which explained American development, but the consensus of opinion among the various interest groups throughout American history over the values and institutions which shaped life in the United States. The so-called consensus historians pointed out that all Americans accepted the basic tenets of American life such as private property and political democracy, and that when conflicts arose they were over the details of how to implement these concepts. Thus, the consensus historians of the forties and fifties rejected the idea that American history had been a series of social clashes and economic confrontations between two groups of antagonists who viewed the nature of society differently. Instead, consensus scholars such as Daniel Boorstin, *The Genius of American Politics* (1953), maintained that the American past was the success story of a pluralistic democratic capitalist society which had been subtly changed to meet the challenges of industrialism by the reforms of the New Deal. In his view, it was difficult to identify heroes and villains, victims and oppressors within the context of our pluralistic history. The conflicts between Whigs and Democrats, Populists and Eastern bankers, Progressives and Conservatives, were not attempts to change the system, but merely the efforts of interest groups to get a larger share of the benefits of American life. Throughout American history, the many interest groups, classes, and factions may have been in conflict, but the consensus scholars claimed that they did not differ on the fundamental structure of American society — they, like children, simply wanted a bigger slice of the pie. By the end of the 1950s, this interpretation of American history, which emphasized the consensus and continuity of our past, dominated historical writing and had its counterparts in the academic fields of political science and sociology. Intellectuals in all areas of study seemed to agree that American democratic, pluralistic institutions represented the best of all possible worlds.

The emergence of the New Left and its radical interpretation of American history was one of the great political and intellectual surprises of the mid-twentieth century. It was totally unexpected because consensus historians dominated their profession to such an extent that it seemed impossible that any group could seriously challenge their interpretation of the American past. Old Left intellectuals, for example, were dispirited by the mid-1950s and their influence within the historical profession was declining. Shocked and puzzled by the reemergence of despotic power in Stalinist Russia, many radical students such as John P. Roche and Martin Diamond soon abandoned Marx's theory of class conflict and embraced the ideas of the consensus historians. Within this context, it appeared highly unlikely that a new radical movement of the Left would emerge to challenge the prevailing consensus view of American society. But the New Left movement did arise suddenly in the late 1950s amidst the quiescent conformism and the political apathy of the decade.

To understand the nature of the New Left revision of American history in the last two decades, it is important to review the origins of this new radical movement. The New Left was at first a political activist group which later sought to reinterpret American history in order to provide a basis for its reformist ideas. The "Movement" was born in deed, not in doctrine. New Left activists, mainly of the younger generation, were reacting against the American society of the fifties which they considered to be an antiseptic wasteland of stucco and plastic. They shared the "Beat Poet's" view that the 1950s had become "an air-conditioned nightmare." In the early 1960s many young college students read and absorbed Paul Goodman's *Growing Up Absurd* (1960) which pointed out how ineffective the new affluent society was in providing meaningful work for its youth. Goodman rebuked Americans for being self-congratulatory and content within a political system which fostered racism, war, and poverty. Young people, Goodman insisted, were becoming increasingly alienated from a society which was complacent and rigid in the face of growing social and economic problems. C. Wright Mills, a sociologist from Columbia University, also refused to go along with the consensus view of American life. In *The Power Elite* (1956), he maintained that a small group of men from the socially prominent families of the nation ran America. Although the reality of American life was hidden under an egalitarian ideology and formal democracy, this elite group governed a class society made up of the rulers and the ruled. Thus Mills, like Goodman, rejected the arguments of the consensus scholars who emphasized pluralism and continuity in American society.

During the late fifties and early sixties, tens of thousands of college students who read the works of Goodman, Mills, and Herbert Marcuse's *One-Dimensional Man* (1964) became more conscious of class conflict and alienation in American life. Radicalized students organized campus groups such as the Students For A Democratic Society (SDS) to combat the social and economic problems which their elders had largely ignored. In 1960, students took the lead in attacking the racial caste system in America by organizing sit-ins and freedom rides in the heart of the deep South. The Student Nonviolent Coordinating Committee (SNCC) played an important role in the civil rights movement throughout the 1960s. Influenced by Michael Harrington's *The Other America* (1963), student leaders also pointed to the inhumanity and inequities in a society which tolerated widespread poverty in a nation of plenty. High school seniors and college freshmen who read *The Other America* discovered the "invisible poor," a class which had been exploited and forgotten by the American ruling elite. The assassination of President Kennedy in 1963, moreover, brought anguish and despair to many young Americans who had seen a glimmer of hope for the future in Kennedy's youthful vigor. His shocking death caused many students to move from passivity to activism in the hope of creating a new society to replace the corrupt, moribund system of the present. An increasing number of young students rejected American history as it had been taught to them and dated the beginning of past events in 1963. In assessing the importance of Kennedy's assassination, one student stated that, "for me this one act has made all other acts irrelevant and trivial, it has replaced time with paranoia, good with evil, relative simplicity with incomprehensibility, and ideal with dirt." By the mid-sixties, a small activist youth movement, fueled by the writing of nonorthodox social critics, had emerged to challenge the prevailing pluralistic, consensus view of American life both present and past.

The New Left movement, which lacked a central focus, a coherent ideology, and a useable past might have burned itself out in the course of the sixties had it not been for the Vietnam War. For many young Americans, the war symbolized all of the evils that were inherent in the American political system. It demonstrated the greed and inhumanity of American leaders who were attempting to subdue a rising nationalist movement in far-off Asia. For the New Left, the war was a class struggle between a capitalist, *status quo* power, the United States, and a dynamic socialist nation, North Vietnam, which represented the aspirations of the peasants and the workers. New Left orators denounced the Vietnam War as a conflict which exposed the exploitive nature of American capitalism. The American ruling class supported the war, according to New Left leaders, in order to provide an outlet for American economic expansion without coming to grips with the serious social and economic problems which existed at home. What was worse, the capitalist power elite attempted to rationalize the American presence in Vietnam by explaining it in terms of the United States' mission to defend freedom and democracy all over the globe. New Left leaders such as Tom Hayden of the SDS denounced the war as a fraud and a travesty which violated the principles upon which America was founded.

In the mid-sixties the antiwar movement grew as a result of the dramatic escalation of American involvement in the Asian conflict. Vietnam provided the central focus which unified the New Left movement and made it a powerful force in American politics. By the mid-sixties, the New Left had expanded its base of support beyond the college campuses and drew new members from among the middle class and the academic intellectuals. The growth of the movement, however, exposed one of the serious weaknesses of the New Left which youthful college students had been willing to ignore. The New Left had no creditable ideology or interpretation of history which might legitimatize its existence and make it attractive to nonstudent groups. Intellectuals, who had either inspired or later joined the movement, attempted to fill this void by providing a usable interpretation of American history which would explain the basis for New Left activism. It was mainly for this reason that the New Left interpretation of the American experience emerged in the early 1960s to challenge the dominant consensus viewpoint.

The New Left view of history was based on an ideological framework that was outlined by the neo-Marxist philosopher, Herbert Marcuse. Marcuse stressed the early writings of Marx which emphasized "humanism" rather than the later Marx of

Das Kapital (1867) which set forth the theory of economic determinism. For Marcuse, the crime of capitalism was not primarily economic; it was cultural and aesthetic. The masses in the advanced western capitalist societies as well as in the "state capitalist" system of the Soviet Union were exploited and alienated, but they did not know it because the ruling elite had imposed upon them a "false consciousness" which obscured their "true consciousness." The exploited masses had come to love their prison, Marcuse maintained, because the state provided bread and circuses and partially satisfied the false wants created by advertising. According to Marcuse, this type of exploitation which existed in industrial societies was not the crude economic deprivation which Marx had prophesied in 1867. It was alienation from love and work. Yet all this was hidden from the masses by a system of propaganda, miseducation, and manipulation. Marcuse believed that this subtle form of exploitation and bondage imposed on the masses justified a revolution against the system in the name of the masses. It is interesting to note that the neo-Marxists of the New Left were almost as critical and contemptuous of the Old Left as they were of the bourgeois leaders. For them, the Old Left had become too doctrinaire and bureaucratic. Old line Marxists continued to emphasize the economic exploitation and deprivation of the workers — themes that missed the mark in describing the alienation which existed in advanced industrial societies. The New Left agreed that economic factors were vital in the historical process, but they were more flexible in their analysis of the exploitation and alienation which afflicted modern man. New Left interpretations of American history reflect this flexibility. The new radical historians, in contrast to the Old Left, are not the captives of an official ideology.

In view of the importance of the Vietnam War to the new radical movement, it is not surprising that the first area of concern for New Left scholars was American foreign policy and more specifically the Cold War conflict. The first serious challenge to the Traditional or orthodox interpretation of United States diplomatic history came from William A. Williams of the University of Wisconsin. Williams, who had been trained in mathematics and the physical sciences as well as in history, joined the faculty at Wisconsin in 1957 and established relations with a thriving New Left community there. In 1959, a number of Williams' students including James Weinstein and Lloyd Gardner founded *Studies on the Left*, a journal committed to the New Left cause. The object of the journal and the New Left historians who contributed to it, was to *"Americanize the radical program* by bringing historically native radicalism up to date."* New Left scholars such as Williams accepted what was needed from Marxist theory insofar as it applied to American history. But Williams and his students, following the lead of Marcuse, emphasized the early "soft" Marx who spoke in terms of alienation rather than the later "hard" Marx of *Das Kapital* who stressed the class struggle and the economic submersion of the proletariat. By carefully sifting from Marxist theory those ideas that were applicable to the American experience, Williams constructed a neo-Marxist interpretation of United States foreign policy in *The Tragedy of American Diplomacy* (1959).

Williams attacked the Traditionalist or orthodox view of American foreign relations which the consensus historians of the 1950s had embraced and refined. Orthodox diplomatic historians held that since its founding the United States had attempted to withdraw and isolate itself from foreign involvements. Taking heed of George Washington's warning about the danger of international entanglements, nineteenth century American leaders avoided unnecessary interaction in European affairs. According to the Traditionalists, America became a model republic which stood as a shining example for the rest of the world to emulate; it was neither corrupt, bellicose, nor imperialistic. Traditionalists agreed, however, that in the 1890s the United States strayed from its steady isolationalist, anticolonial policy and became engaged, almost accidently, in the Spanish-American War which led to the acquisition of American colonies. From the orthodox perspective, this adventure in imperialism was an aberration. Realizing their mistake, American policymakers quickly reverted to the older policy of isolationism and antiimperialism. The United States retained its colonies, but became increasingly determined not to stumble into an imperialist war in the future. During the twentieth century, the Traditionalists argued, American leaders committed the nation to a foreign policy which emphasized isolationism and anticolonialism. The Traditionalist maintained that the United States only reluctantly entered World Wars I and II to defend the principles of freedom and democracy against the forces of totalitarianism. Similarly, the American response to the Soviet challenge in the Cold War period was, as one orthodox historian put it, "the brave and essential response of free men to communist aggression." From this point of view, the American involvement in the Korean and Vietnam wars had been an attempt to defend free nations from the aggressive, expansionist tenacles of the world Communist movement. With a few minor exceptions, consensus historians adopted this Traditionalist interpretation which defended American diplomacy in the twentieth century as a courageous effort to maintain isolationist principles, but flexible enough to defend democratic ideals in times of crisis.

Williams and his followers viewed the American diplomatic tradition quite differently. The New Left revisionists maintained that the United States had always been an expansionist nation continuously pushing westward in pursuit of economic opportunity. They charged that the orthodox historians overlooked America's imperialistic impulse because most of the new territory acquired in the pre-Civil War period had been taken from Indians or European colonial nations. The revisionists further maintained, however, that "Manifest Destiny" was simply another form of imperialism. In *The Tragedy of American Diplomacy*, Williams argued that American foreign policy had been aggressive and imperialistic from the very beginning. Westward expansion, he pointed out, brought about continued economic opportunities for American capitalists and allowed them to prosper without having to confront the basic social and economic problems which the system bred. Williams, like Frederick J. Turner, believed that the frontier acted like a safety valve in releasing the pressures of urban discontent which were the inevitable by-product of the exploitive capitalist economy. But when the frontier area was nearly exhausted by the 1890s, Williams argued, American leaders acted on behalf of the capitalist interests in searching for new overseas frontiers which might be utilized to relieve the pressures of unemployment, low pay, and substandard working conditions which were prevalent at home. Williams claimed that American capitalists hoped that the overseas colonies, acquired as a result of the Spanish-American War, might provide the markets, raw materials, and impetus for economic expansion which the frontier had created for previous generations. Thus,

Williams viewed American imperialism in the 1890s not as an aberration or accident, but as the natural outgrowth of the capitalist-controlled diplomatic policies of the United States.

In analyzing American diplomacy in the early twentieth century, Williams maintained that there was a fundamental change in strategy. American leaders, he stated, recognized the shortcomings and dangers involved in maintaining a colonial empire. The overseas possessions were not only expensive to support and difficult to defend, but the very idea of formal colonialism ran counter to America's revolutionary heritage. It was for this reason, Williams contended, that the United States turned away from European-style imperialism and embraced a policy of overseas economic expansion based on the Open Door. According to Williams, the Open Door was and is the central theme of American diplomacy in the twentieth century because it represents the attempt of American policymakers to resolve the internal contradictions of capitalism — chronic overproduction, unemployment, depression — without fundamentally changing the system itself. Originally applied to China, the Open Door policy called for the free and equal access to economic opportunities for all nations everywhere in the world. Under this doctrine, America's powerful and efficient economic system might expand to all corners of the globe and dominate lesser developed societies without resorting to the unpleasant methods of European-style imperialism.

Williams conceded that the Open Door policy, which quickly evolved from a utopian idea into an ideology, was a stroke of genius by American policymakers. But it led to a tragic era for America. During the course of the twentieth century, Williams argued, American leaders enlarged the Open Door into a worldwide policy, defining any attempt to obstruct this goal as a threat to the American system which was based on the need for unhindered expansion. As Williams put it, the Open Door was an attempt to evade domestic problems by "embarking on crusades to save everybody else." Most Traditional historians failed to perceive the nature of American diplomacy, Williams maintained, because policymakers "internalized" the Open Door concept and usually found discussion of it unnecessary, even among themselves. By the early part of the century, the United States had developed what Williams called a system of "corporate state radicalism" — an apparently liberal regime, which was actually dominated by the larger corporations and capitalist banking interests. Under this system, America rapidly became an over-centralized and outwardly aggressive state; a nation which had violated its founding principles and threatened other nations in the world.

During the 1960s, Williams' students and other New Left scholars attempted to document the Open Door interpretation of American foreign policy. Walter LaFeber, *The New Empire* (1963), wrote that America's venture into imperialism in the 1890s was neither a historical accident nor a new departure. It was the culmination of a process dating at least to the 1850s and 1860s which sprang from the need for raw materials and markets. N. Gordon Levin, *Woodrow Wilson and World Politics* (1968), reinterpreted Wilson's post-World War I diplomacy. He rejected the Traditional view that Wilson's wartime objective to "make the world safe for democracy" was simply a policy designed to spread participatory government and representative institutions to the rest of the world. According to Levin, Wilson was mainly talking about the expansion of American economic influence; that is, making the world safe for United States trade and investments abroad. In treating the 1930s, Lloyd Gardner, *Economic Aspects of New Deal Diplomacy* (1964), concluded that following the domestic economic setbacks of 1937-38, American leaders abandoned reform in pursuit of world frontiers as a solution to the crisis of the decade. Gardner suggested that America's entrance into World War II, which had been applauded by Old Left scholars, was an attempt to impose liberal trade and the Open Door on the reluctant Axis powers.

The most thoroughgoing revision of the Traditional interpretation of American diplomacy by New Left scholars, however, has centered on the more timely issue of the origins of the Cold War. A group of revisionist historians including Gabriel Kolko, Diane Clemens, and Gar Alperovitz wrote monographs during the 1960s challenging the orthodox view that the Cold War began as a result of the aggressive, expansionist policies of Soviet Marxists. Turning the story around, New Left scholars emphasized the aggressive and expansionistic strategy of the United States in contrast to the more limited objectives of Russia at the end of World War II. They maintained that Joseph Stalin had resolved the contradiction between "the expansive prophecy of Marx about world revolution" and "a realistic

Marxian analysis of world conditions" in the most conservative manner. The Soviet leader was adamant on only three postwar objectives; that Russia have friendly governments to her West, that she have the reparations and/or loans to rebuild her economy, and that she have a guarantee that Germany would not be able to rearm. New Left historians claimed that all other issues confronting Russia and the United States were negotiable and that had American policymakers agreed to the Soviet war aims, there need not have been an intense Cold War struggle. Instead, the revisionists maintained, United States officials, in their quest for an Open Door in Eastern Europe, opposed the Soviet objective in that region and subsequently mapped a strategy which threatened the other two minimum demands of the Russians. The United States, therefore, in the New Left view, was mainly responsible for the Cold War by adopting an aggressive policy through which the Americans attempted to block the Soviet Union from achieving her modest postwar goals — goals that were mainly defensive rather than aggressive in nature. This interpretation of the origins of the Cold War served as the intellectual basis for the antiwar movement of the 1960s and 1970s, which stressed the immoral and aggressive nature of the American involvement in Vietnam.

Despite the preeminence of foreign policy issues in the 1960s, New Left historians did not limit their criticism of American society to diplomatic affairs. New Left activists and revisionist historians alike, maintained that there was a vital link between America's expansionist foreign policy and the decay and destruction of American institutions and political liberties. The pursuit of the Open Door in foreign policy, combined with the resistance of many nations to this objective, forced the United States to expand and centralize its government. In the process, according to revisionist scholars, the ruling capitalist elite wrested economic power away from the people and concentrated it in its own hands. The revisionists maintained that Traditional historians failed to recognize this fundamental change in American society because the capitalist ruling class retained the trappings of a liberal representative government while they, in fact, controlled the government. In examining recent domestic affairs, Gabriel Kolko, *Main Currents In Modern American History* (1976), stated that capitalism is "the very bedrock of modern American history — the overriding structure which predetermines the purposes for which the United States exists today." He told a story of rule by elites, with business leaders being the most important group, the masses ignored and manipulated, military men the faithful servants, and the government utilized for economic purposes.

Kolko and other revisionists used these main themes in rewriting American domestic history in the twentieth century. They rejected the consensus view that American big business had been controlled and regulated as a result of progressive reform movements. The Progressive Era, 1900-1917, and the New Deal, 1933-1940, had been cited by consensus and many socio-economic historians as being successful efforts by government to harness the increasing power of large corporations. In *The Triumph of Conservatism* (1963), Kolko attempted to show that the alleged middle class-inspired reforms of the Progressive Era were a fraud. Kolko along with James Weinstein and Robert Wiebe maintained that the so-called reforms, supposedly designed to regulate big business, were really engineered by the businessmen themselves to prevent destructive competition. According to New Left historians, the major Progressive reform acts — the Meat Inspection Act, the Federal Reserve Act, the Federal Trade Commission Act — were initiated by meat packers, bankers, and businessmen respectively. Kolko, the most strident critic of the orthodox view of the Progressive era, also maintained that "the railroads, not the farmers or shippers, were the most important single advocates of federal legislation from 1877 to 1916." He and his radical colleagues attacked both Theodore Roosevelt and Woodrow Wilson, the heroes of the consensus historians, for being the tools of the industrial elite. In fact, the New Left studies of political reforms in the early twentieth century turned the consensus interpretation of the Progressive Era on its head. The revisionist scholars concluded that the Progressive Era was not an urban middle class reform movement, but instead the triumph of conservative capitalism.

The New Left studies of the New Deal followed the same general pattern as those on the earlier reform movement. In *The New Deal* (1967), Paul Conkin maintained that the reform era under Franklin Roosevelt was goalless and aimless without either moral or practical purposes. Other revisionists charged that the New Deal did not address itself to the fundamental structural problems which had resulted from the domination of the society by conservative capitalist interests. Roosevelt was basically conservative, they claimed, and he did little more than treat the human consequences of the economic collapse with relief and the alphabet agencies: PWA, WPA, AAA, and CCC. The revisionists also maintained that many of Roosevelt's "reform" measures were beneficial to banking and business interests. The National Recovery Act (1933), for example, stamped out competition and allowed each industry to set its own prices and production codes. In general, New Left historians contend that the New Deal "reforms" helped to accelerate the political centralization process which had begun in the Progressive Era. Roosevelt failed to seize the opportunity to create a truly cooperative society, they point out, and in the process of drifting aimlessly from one panacea to the next, helped to father a massive welfare state controlled by a capitalist elite. According to the New Left, the New Deal was the spawning ground for the economically overcentralized and outwardly aggressive nation which America is today.

The vigorous New Left criticism of United States diplomatic and domestic history has not gone unchallenged. Many orthodox historians have criticized the New Left for using history as a weapon to further its cause in the contemporary political struggles in American society. The revisionists, they say, show contempt for pure history, history that is written without reference to the present cultural and political issues. Most orthodox scholars maintain that useful historical studies result from a detachment from contemporary causes and an attempt to maintain political neutrality on the issues or events being examined. From the consensus viewpoint, New Left books are documents of propaganda which speak more to current political debates than to the problems of the past. Although the early orthodox criticism of the New Left historians was often moderate and indulgent, the recent attacks on the revisionist scholars have been more strident and provocative. This increasingly hostile reaction to the revisionist interpretations and methodology by consensus historians was triggered by the proliferation of New Left studies in the late sixties and early seventies purporting to show that the United States was mainly responsible for the Cold War. Clearly the preeminence of the Vietnam debate during that period raised the ire of orthodox historians who believed that the New Left was distorting history to bolster the antiwar movement and undermine the authority of the duly constituted government.

The most outspoken critic of the New Left is Robert J. Maddox, who has written numerous articles and a book, *The New Left And The Origins Of The Cold War* (1973), attacking the revisionists and their methodology. He maintained that the New Left historians have done untold injury to historical scholarship by violating basic accepted rules in the use of evidence in their books on the Cold War. After carefully checking the footnotes in seven revisionist monographs for the period between February and August 1945, a period including both the Yalta and Potsdam conferences, Maddox concluded that New Left historians not only failed to provide any evidence to document their interpretation but, in fact, manufactured their own evidence. Maddox charged that William A. Williams in *The Tragedy of American Diplomacy* "frequently constructed imaginary speeches and dialogues by splicing together phrases uttered at different times and on diverse subjects." For Maddox, the real "tragedy" was that Williams' book "has been taken seriously by those who ought to have known better." He leveled similar charges against the other revisionist writers of the Cold War period. Maddox maintained that Gabriel Kolko's *Politics of War* (1968), like the other New Left monographs, was a hodgepodge of factual errors and false interpretations which frequently rested upon a grotesque rendition of documentary materials.

During the ongoing debate between consensus and revisionist historians, the New Left has launched a vigorous counterattack against its orthodox critics. Their common defense has been that Maddox and his colleagues, perhaps caught in the grips of some kind of neo-McCarthy hysteria, have simply confused the concepts of interpretation and falsification. They categorically deny that they have created or falsified historical evidence and, in turn, have accused Maddox and his supporters of trumping up the charges against them by quoting out of context and by using shoddy historical methodology themselves. During the past few years the criticism and countercriticism surrounding the Cold War controversy and other areas of New Left revisionism has degenerated into a round of name-calling and mudslinging unmatched in historical circles since the Beard-Tansill-Barnes revisionist studies after World War II which purported to show that President Roosevelt deliberately left Pearl Harbor undefended in 1941 in order to provoke a Japanese attack.

One moderate-to-left diplomatic historian, Warren Kimball of Rutgers University, has urged both the New Left and its extreme critics to tone down the personal attacks which they have launched against each other, lest the current crop of graduate students emulate their mentors and drive the historical profession into polarized camps. He argued that the Cold War controversy is mainly one of conflicting interpretation rather than a conscious effort on the part of the New Left to distort history. Kimball predicted that this dispute, like historical controversies of the past, will moderate as a new generation of scholars attempt to synthesize the seemingly irreconcilable points of view. If this does occur, the New Left interpretation of American history, which became so prominent and provocative in the 1960s and early 1970s, will be relegated to a lesser position in the historian's collection of diverse viewpoints of the past. The ebbing of the New Left interpretation within the historical community would not be surprising in that the earlier socioeconomic and consensus view of the American experience have been revised, refined, and synthesized during the past three decades. New Left historians will probably meet the fate of their predecessors as the constant revising and rewriting of American history continues in the coming decades.

But the New Left revisionists deserve praise for their effort to explore new paths and enrich our perspective of the past. Their work has added a new dimension to the study of American history and it serves as a useful corrective to the self-congratulatory interpretations of the postwar consensus historians. Despite their strident criticism of the New Left interpretations and methodology, orthodox historians will be forced to reexamine their own assumptions and methods as a result of the questions raised by the radical revisionists. In the area of foreign policy, the New Left has shown that American diplomacy is not always motivated by high ideals and global humanitarianism. America, like any country, is driven by diverse interests including economic and political self-interest. In general, the revisionists have forced orthodox diplomatic historians to review the entire course of American foreign relations with a more critical eye. In addition, the New Left has exposed domestic problems which consensus historians of the fifties had conveniently overlooked. In the wake of the New Left revisionism, it is doubtful that historians in the future will applaud democratic capitalism without taking note of the revisionist questions concerning the very basis of the American economic and political system. The New Left revisionists, despite their present-mindedness and debatable historical methods, have raised questions about the American past which need to be answered. The influence of the New Left historians might recede, but their contribution to the study of American history cannot be denied. They have raised new questions and offered new explanations, and that is after all what the study of history is all about.

SUGGESTED READINGS

In addition to those books cited in the essay, the reader should consult John S. Bassett, *Middle Group of American Historians* (1917), Marcus Cunliffe and Robin W. Winks, eds., *Pastmasters: Essays on American Historians* (1969), and Harvey Wish, ed., *The American Historian* (1960) for an introduction to Traditional historians. On the Progressive or socioeconomic historians, the two best introductory works are Richard Hofstadter, *The Progressive Historians: Turner, Beard, and Parrington* (1968) and Lee Benson, *Turner and Beard: Reconsidered* (1960). Two articles, John Higham, "Cult of American Consensus," *Commentary*, 27 (1959) and Rogers Hollingsworth, "Consensus and Continuity in Historical Writing," *South Atlantic Quarterly*, 61 (1962), serve as an excellent introduction to the consensus viewpoint. Already, there are a large number of books on the New Left Movement. The best works are James Weinstein, *Ambiguous Legacy: The Left in American Politics* (1975), Theodore Roszak, *The Making of a Counterculture: Reflections on the Technocratic Society and Its Youthful Opposition* (1969), Irwin Unger, *The Movement: A History of the American New Left 1959-1972* (1974), and Edward Bacciocco, Jr., *The New Left in America: Reform to Revolution, 1956-1970* (1974). For an interpretation of some New Left historians see Irwin Unger, "The 'New Left' and American History: Some Recent Trends in United States Historiography", *American Historical Review*, 72 (July 1967).

AMERICAN INDUSTRY AND SOCIETY

RAPID INDUSTRIAL AND URBAN DEVELOPMENT have wrought enormous changes in the fabric of American society since the latter nineteenth century. Rural villages and family-owned enterprises have steadily given way to sprawling metropolises and multinational corporations. In 1860 only about 20 percent of the American people lived in urban areas; by 1970 the figure was almost 75 percent. Even the traditionally rural and agricultural South has become urbanized, with about 65 percent of its residents now residing in cities.

The urbanization of American society has been fostered by industrialization in general and accelerated by the automobile in particular. As aptly described by Professor Walter Sutton, the impact of the automobile upon American life has been breathtaking. Indeed, it is difficult today to imagine American culture without the car. But Professor Sutton does more than recount the American love affair with the automobile. He calls attention to problems spawned by the auto industry. Despite growing concern about energy resources and soaring fuel prices, however, Professor Sutton optimistically concludes that the car culture will endure. Viewing industrialization from another perspective, Professor Dale Royalty traces the growth of corporations from United States Steel to the multinationals. Professor Royalty not only describes how this process has affected farmers and laborers, but also explains the interrelationship between economic objectives and political policies, especially foreign policy.

Alterations in the physical configuration of society have been paralleled by intellectual adjustments. As Professor John W. Storey writes, nineteenth century Americans, guided by the church and/or reason, generally presupposed the existence of universal laws underlying the movement of history. But twentieth century Americans, given the influence of pragmatic relativism and Freudian and behavioral psychology, have become less certain. While Professor Storey emphasizes intellectual change, he detects in American behavior a degree of continuity. So despite the enormous changes of the past century, Professor Storey questions whether or not American character has undergone drastic modification.

While the corporation and automobile have been vehicles of change, the South, as a region, has experienced vast economic and social alterations since the Civil War. Although the South remained predominantly rural until after World War II, the leadership of the post-Civil War New South was committed to industrialization and urbanization. And as Professor M. B. Lucas indicates, those objectives have been virtually accomplished. Economically vibrant and politically influential, the South today occupies an enviable position — a fact demonstrated by the continuing migration of business firms and people to the so-called Sun Belt.

Another problem not yet solved. (Eastern Pennsylvania, 1935)
(Library of Congress)

CHAPTER ONE

The Influence of the Automobile

WALTER A. SUTTON

Over the last decade Americans have come to realize that the automobile has had a greater impact on our lives, our cities, and our nation than any other force of our time with the possible exception of electricity. Americans have come to realize that this impact, especially during the last decade, has been harmful. Yet few Americans know much about the history of the automobile or of its impact; few know that by the 1920s many of the problems which we face today had already appeared and were ignored.

The first autos which could be called commercial successes appeared in Germany about 1886; they were the tricycles of Karl Benz and Gottlieb Daimler. Soon production spread to France and the rest of Europe and then across the Atlantic to the United States, where several dozen backyard mechanics were active by 1894. The successful tinkerers had cars ready for sale by 1896, and the Stanley twins, the Duryea brothers, and Elwood P. Haynes marketed primitive horseless carriages before the turn of the century. By 1900 some 3500 vehicles had been sold by about six makers, not one of whom was Henry Ford, who is often credited by the ignorant with building the first car. Many of the early buyers were doctors who found the car more reliable than the horse when making their rounds. Others were rich men who liked expensive toys. Between 1900 and 1910 hundreds of companies entered the business, at least briefly, and the giants were producing over 10,000 cars apiece in 1910. Those giants included Cadillac, Buick, Studebaker, and Ford, with Ford's being the largest maker in the world. By 1917 Ford was producing 622,000 cars a year, about as many as all other American car makers put together. The automobile revolution had begun.

Most early automobile companies usually aimed their products at the rich, and many cars cost over a thousand dollars at a time when the average middle class family made only that much in a single year. Several producers, however, realized the enormous potential of cheaper cars. Ransom E. Olds' curved-dash Oldsmobile of 1901 was the first vehicle to be made by mass production techniques in an effort to lower production costs. Priced at $650, the Merry Olds was a light, flimsy horseless carriage, not well suited to the miserable roads of that time. Still it was cheap and popular. Another maker to use similar construction techniques was Henry M. Leland, whose Cadillac was built to high standards and sold well despite its $800 or $900 (later $1500) cost. Billy Durant, the creator of General Motors, also attempted mass production of moderately priced Buicks. Despite the success of Olds, Leland, and Durant, the man whose name is always associated with cheaper cars and the assembly line is Henry Ford.

Ford had a problem in securing the approval of his partners for the production of a cheap car, but when he succeeded, that car, the Model T, made history and made Ford the most admired man of his time. Introduced in 1908 and priced at $850, the T was strongly built of first class materials and its high wheels could go nearly anywhere. Its design was so simple that the average owner could make most repairs. Furthermore, almost anyone could afford the T because Ford always used the latest mass production methods to lower the cost. By 1927, its last year of production, the cheapest T sold for $290.

Ford was not an educated man; he, like many of the early car makers, was self-taught. He had not read the works of Frederick W. Taylor, who provided the theory behind mass production. But his subordinates had, and they used them to develop the manufacturing techniques which revolutionized not just the auto industry, but many other industries as well.

Ford quickly grasped the ultimate logic of the moving production line: Increased productivity meant lowered costs and selling prices. Ford decided in 1914 to raise the minimum wage at his plants to five dollars a day, an action possible because mass production reduced the labor force. At a time when most workmen made one or two dollars a day, Ford's action created a national furor. Businessmen laughed at the insanity of the act, but workmen came to Detroit by the thousands to try to get jobs at Ford. At the same time that Ford raised wages, he reduced the selling price of the T to $600, still making huge profits. Ford hoped that the well-paid worker would buy the Model T. If workers could not afford consumer products, he reasoned, the makers would go bankrupt. In other words, pay a man a decent wage and he will buy your products, the basis of the consumer economy. Credit purchase of cars evolved about the same time, further increasing consumerism and car ownership. The Ford Motor Company and the entire automotive industry quickly became a potent force in the American economy.

The Model T was a source of much humor. Everyone told Ford jokes, and several magazines devoted to them appeared. One magazine asked, for example, what time is it when two T's meet? Tin past tin. Ford could never have bought so much favorable publicity. Nor could he have bought the coverage given in 1927 to the new Model A. Its introduction ranked with Lindbergh's flight in the amount of space devoted to it by the newspapers. Millions came to the showrooms across the country to see the new cars. The A, however, did not have nearly the great success that came to the T. It was discontinued after four years, when Ford adopted the three-year body cycle already introduced by General Motors and still continuing today. Under this system, the consumer had to pay for the new planned obsolescence.

Ford quickly became the rarest of all Americans, the hero-millionaire. For farmers Ford was the man who freed them from drudgery, and for urbanites he was the man who gave them mobility. Yet Ford was more than a hero; he was the symbol of his age. Standing with one foot in the past and one foot in the present, Ford personified the ambivalence of the 1920s. He prized the small town and its imagined virtues, and he admired modern technology. At his Greenfield Village and Ford Museum he tried both to re-create the perfect nineteenth century small town and to show the importance of invention, especially concentrating on the work of his friend, Thomas A. Edison. Ford did not seem to realize that the Model T was doing more than any other force to destroy the placid life which he so much esteemed.

Although the Model T and many other early cars could go almost anywhere, early motorists soon came to realize that the nation needed better roads. Yes, they could concentrate all their driving in the city with good streets, but how boring that was. They wanted to get out on the open, dusty (or muddy) road, even if travel meant dirty faces, filthy clothing, and getting stuck. Inevitably, early auto organizations, and construction companies came to advocate that the states and, especially, the federal government subsidize road building. By 1916 several states had adopted a gasoline tax to raise funds, a method that rapidly became universal, and the federal government had passed its first highway act. It would be decades before even a network of two-lane roads crisscrossed the country, but by the middle 1920s the car owner could take trips into the countryside, although many miles of roads were still graveled. The motoring vacation became common, and drivers frequently traveled hundreds of miles, even across the continent. The roads also helped move the farmer into the twentieth century by substantially reducing his isolation and integrating him into the consumer economy. The car freed America from restrictions made on travel by the horse and the train.

Cars and trucks began to have real impact on America during the midteens; before then there were too few of them to be significant. The bus and tractor appeared soon after. Until the middle 1920s, the motor vehicle was the greatest progressive force in American life, producing social and economic improvement superior to that of all reform legislation combined. The impact was visible the nation over. Farmers began to use tractors to increase their production. Every Saturday the farmer and his family traveled thirty to forty miles to the county seat in their T truck. There they could buy food and supplies for the next week at cheaper prices than at the village general store, and they could also go to the movies. Many farmers would rather spend money on cars than on dry goods, as some merchants complained. And what was true in the country was also true in the city. People wanted cars. Before the car, the nation's towns and cities had to remove tons of manure and thousands of dead horses every year, or at least attempt to remove them. The car eliminated a major cause of disease, a service which all Americans appreciated. They also liked the convenience of easier travel to work, school, or store and quicker delivery of goods. Manufacturers found truck transportation cheaper and better than any other form. The motor vehicle transformed America into a more mobile and efficient society.

It also affected traditional patterns of daily life. People would sacrifice almost anything, even having more children, to own a car. Husbands came to tolerate working wives if the additional income went for a new car, one factor accounting for the increased number of working wives in the 1920s. The automobile became both the symbol of personal mobility and the means of achieving it, an old dream come true. Whether the occupants were families avoiding church to look for pleasure on a Sunday morning or young couples escaping the anxious eyes of parents, whether the occupants were rich or poor (almost anyone could afford a used T), the car brought personal freedom and affected family and society. Children now had a new quarrel with their parents: When could they use the car? Critics might condemn the car for corrupting traditional family life and sexual morality, but they made few converts. The people enjoyed their new freedom.

On the road, the black was equal to the white. Racial segregation could not be the basis of traffic laws. On the road, the car brought status to both blacks and whites who had none at home. With a car, a person, however poor, was somebody. Consequently, while the ordinary American could not afford a Lincoln or a Packard, he sold his Model T as soon as he could buy a better car with more style, and, as the twenties progressed and the design of the T aged, that something better was usually a Chevrolet, priced at $600 and probably bought on credit. Ford lost its lead, never to regain it for long. Status became more important than mere utility.

The car, then, was the cause of significant change in the mores and lives of many Americans. What is the norm today was largely in existence by 1930, and the car was mainly responsible. Not all of the effects were good, as many critics pointed out at the time. Trucks and buses took much business away from the railroads, many of which came to face bankruptcy. Farmers overproduced and suffered falling prices.

Americans, however, seemed able to live with the bad. Suburban sprawl, traffic congestion, deteriorating downtowns, drunk drivers, traffic accidents and deaths, increased taxes, and bigger police forces were all obvious developments of the 1920s. Americans could tolerate the malevolent effects of the car because they felt the good far outweighed the bad. During the early years they were right.

In the 1920s many new automakers entered the industry, and by 1929 it and its directly and indirectly related companies were the largest employers in America. Oil production, service and repair, glass making, lumbering, sheep raising, rubber production, tourist accommodations, and roadside souvenir sales were among the many endeavors dependent upon the car. Yet even before the Great Depression hit in 1930, the industry was in trouble because of market saturation. The Depression brought disaster. Motor travel, gasoline consumption, and car production all declined, and many of the weaker makers went bankrupt. Even some of the best known marques — Pierce Arrow, Stutz, Moon, Cord, and Duesenberg, found few buyers and went out of production. After several years, drivers began to resume their traveling habits, but not their purchasing of new cars. Until the late thirties people either made do with the ones they had or bought used ones, and many seemed ready to give up their houses but not their cars. Indeed, many of the poor who wandered America during the thirties looking for work went by road. The most famous of these wanderers were the Okies, the poor, dispossessed farmers of the Middle West, who were tractored off the land by the machines purchased by banks using AAA subsidies, and who trekked to California in search of money and the better life. John Steinbeck's famous novel *The Grapes of Wrath* (1939) vividly portrays the helplessness of these migrants. Most people during the Depression, however, were not down and out; most were hurt but not ruined by the hard times. They stayed home, driving their cars as usual.

By 1935 traffic congestion around major cities was so intense that state and city planners felt compelled to build wider roads, especially if most of the money could be gotten from the federal government through PWA or WPA, those massive relief grants and projects, or through regular highway programs. Pennsylvania, for example, converted some old railroad trackbed into the Pennsylvania Turnpike and provided a model highway for the rest of the country. In and around New York City, Robert Moses, the famous road builder, created a network of parkways, bridges, and one tunnel to make New York, a nineteenth century city, into a modern city of the car. And also in Los Angeles, *the* city of the car, the first freeway opened in 1940, and the city was well on the way toward becoming the asphalt jungle of the motor age. None of these projects, despite their designers' contentions, did much to reduce congestion, for the new roads were soon as clogged with vehicles as had been the old. Designers, nevertheless, continued to promise that their latest programs would at last end the traffic nightmare. If the auto population had stayed constant, perhaps traffic congestion could have been reduced, but there were always more and more cars.

World War II brought some quick but temporary changes to America's car culture, for the government prohibited the production of new vehicles for the civilian market. It also imposed gasoline rationing and a 35-mile-per-hour speed limit for highway travel to conserve natural rubber, which was in short supply because of the Japanese conquest of the East Indies. America was forced to develop a synthetic rubber industry. If people wanted to travel, they had to turn to the train or the bus and suffer overcrowding and long delays. Some did make motor trips, perhaps using counterfeit gas coupons or buying from the black market. All made do with the vehicles which they owned when the war began or used ones which were available at high prices. On the whole, rationing worked well; people at home enjoyed undergoing hardships, if they were not too hard, to demonstrate solidarity with the boys in khaki. Since there were few consumer goods on the market, most Americans saved their money to buy a new car when the war was over, or a house or some other desirable product. Soldiers and civilians fought the war for democracy, the American way, the girl next door, and a new car. The makers hardly suffered from the restrictions; they got huge contracts for planes, tanks, and trucks and made huge profits. And as the war began to wind down, the industry began to plan for greatly increased sales, and it was not to be disappointed.

When the war was over, America went on a spending binge, and the first thing a family might do was to sign up on several auto dealers' waiting lists, scheming how to bypass the others ahead of them. Many purchasers waited up to a year for delivery and felt lucky that by 1949 the cost of a Ford had only doubled (to $1,600) since 1946. The immediate postwar years were boom times for the auto industry; it could sell anything on four wheels. Furthermore, the postwar years were also boom times for the growth of cities, especially of suburbs, and for new street, freeway, and tollway construction. All the transportation indicators were up, and the future seemed limitless. Soon every family would have a small house and two cars, and would commute on the new roads to work or play, a pattern already established by 1925, but considerably expanded by 1955.

Even the Korean war did not put a damper on the future. The average buyer only had to suffer the embarrassment of having less chrome on his new machine. City and state governments and the construction industry began to lobby for massive federal aid for a new interstate highway system of limited-access roads. These roads would meet the needs of motorists and truckers but, as the plan worked out, destroy passenger railroads and gravely injure mass transportation in the United States by reducing the amount spent on them. But then few were interested enough in mass transit to protest the possible consequences of the interstate system, and most would prefer to drive rather than use the bus or the train. Furthermore, few foresaw the social consequences of tearing up huge portions of cities for freeways without providing alternate housing for people whose apartments were torn down. Few foresaw that the interstate system and other freeways would contribute greatly to urban disintegration, to rapid decentralization, and to ugly strip development combined with decaying central cities.

In 1956 Congress created the interstate highway system and a highway trust fund to pay for it. The money would come from taxes on oil products, trucks, and buses. The Eisenhower administration supported the legislation as did special interest groups. After twenty years and tens of billions of dollars spent, the system is still not completed. And the trust-fund advocates, until 1976, blocked spending part of the revenue for mass transit as many have proposed in recent years. Initially many existing tollways and freeways were incorporated into the system, roads which were originally started by the states or state-created authorities. Other freeways have been built under state and other federal programs, and cities receiving revenue-sharing funds have also done much road construction with them. The federal government has become the largest road builder in history, and the end is not yet in sight.

The interstate system and freeways generally have traditionally been planned by engineers who have given little thought to the social consequences of their creations. The road had to go where geography and economics dictated, regardless of what was in the way. At first few complained except for the urban poor who were dispossessed, but nobody important listened to them. By the mid-1960s more audible protests emerged. For example, many citizens in New Orleans objected to a freeway which would have cut the French Quarter off from the Mississippi River, and they succeeded in stopping construction. Yet protests of several environmental groups at running a freeway through San Antonio's Breckenridge Park, the largest in the city, failed. Very few protests were ever made at the location of freeways in rural areas, except where famous beauty spots were threatened as was New Hampshire's Old Man of the Mountain, a natural, stone formation. In recent years, the protest movement against freeways has weakened, perhaps because most of them have been completed or at least are already under construction. One also suspects that younger engineers are also more aware of public opinion and are not so arrogant as their predecessors when planning routes.

Even today highway construction increases. In 1977, the state of Texas spent its considerable surplus not on education or mass transit but on roads. Clearly the highway lobby composed of construction companies and automakers is still powerful, but the time has come for a reassessment of priorities. There are more serious concerns than new roads.

The mid-1950s were the heyday of the freeway and of the big car. Hardly anyone worried about safety, pollution, or increased prices. When Ford tried to sell safety late in the decade, the result was disaster. The public turned to makes promising more power. There has always been a debate between the industry which claims that it only builds what the public wants and its critics who say that the industry educates its customers to buy what is available by shrewdly worded advertisements. Neither position is completely wrong. Beginning in 1949 the industry began to make bigger and more powerful automobiles, constantly restyling them in more and more flamboyant ways (huge tail fins were one result), loading them with options, and advertising them with promises of sex and position. A car's price doubled by 1960 to 3,000 or 4,000 dollars, for the consumer had to pay for the retooling, and he did. The smaller companies, Kaiser-Frazier, Packard, Studebaker, and Hudson, had low sales, could not afford huge costs, and one by one began to go under. The only small firm to remain was American Motors, a combination of Nash and Hudson, and it often lost money. Most Americans until the late 1950s seemed to want or were taught to want, their own fins and tricolored fantasies on wheels. Only a few people desired smaller cars, and they bought Ramblers from American Motors or one of the imported cars which Detroit chose to ignore because large cars brought greater profits.

Very few cars were imported into America before the late 1940s when the sports car craze began and enthusiasts turned to MG, Jaguar, Austin Healey, Triumph, and Mercedes. Then came the Volkswagen, and Detroit had to notice that by 1956 an increasing number of purchasers were prepared to wait for six to nine months for delivery or to pay premium prices for slightly used VW's. About that same time Ford tried to introduce the ultimate middle-class dream machine, the Edsel, and lost a 100 million dollars, for the public did not want it. An increasing number were hoping for an alternative which Detroit could or would not produce.

The success of the VW caused other European makers, notably BMC, Fiat, and Renault, to try to enter the American market for small sedans. To improve sales after the recession of 1958 the Big Three introduced the Ford Falcon, the Chevy Corvair, and the Plymouth Valiant, each costing $2200 stripped. Most of the new foreign car companies could not compete with the compacts and quickly retreated, but VW sales increased. VW had an advantage, a widespread dealer organization. The same cycle was repeated in the late 1960s, for American compacts became larger and more costly; consequently, the Japanese Datsun and Toyota began to increase their market, especially in California where their combined sales in 1971 were greater than either Ford's or Chevrolet's. So Detroit got busy again with another round of smaller cars, the sub-compacts: Pintos, Vegas, Mustang II's.

As the mid '70s arrived, American cars began to grow smaller, but foreign producers continued to sell even larger numbers. With the continuing oil shortage, there will be no reversion to the huge bath tubs of the past. All American makers are scaling down the size of their large cars if not their prices. The carefree day of huge, powerful machines is gone, and, although many regret their disappearance, these cars are obsolete. While many may still be able to afford them, society cannot.

The cost and size of cars is not the only issue; too many still die in accidents. In the early 1960s a concern for the lack of car safety led Ralph Nader, the self-appointed consumer advocate, to publish *Unsafe at any Speed: The Designed-in Dangers of the American Automobile* (1965), containing an attack on the rear-engined Chevrolet Corvair, whose handling was tricky. Nader's polemic, despite many faults, caused great public consciousness of the need for more safety in order to reduce injury and death rates. (Most accidents are caused by bad or drunk drivers, but safer cars can help.) In 1964 the federal government began to set safety standards for the cars which it purchased. The uproar produced by Nader led the Congress to consider setting general standards. During the resulting hearings Nader revealed that GM had hired private detectives to search out incriminating evidence on him. GM publicly apologized and paid Nader $425,000 in damages. The scandal destroyed any chance of Detroit's avoiding safety standards.

In 1966 for the first time the federal government began to mandate safety standards for all cars sold in America, and every year the standards have become more stringent. Beginning with add-ons like seat belts and padded dashes and visors, the industry is now required to build crash-proof bumpers, door locks, gasoline tanks, and steering columns. But seat belt interlocks caused such great public protest in 1974 that they were quickly eliminated. Ford may have been right when it said that safety does not sell. Because many drivers, perhaps two-thirds, refused to wear the belts, the government authorized experiments with air bags, balloons which rapidly expand in case of collision to cushion the occupants from harm. Although the safety harness is far superior, the government has now required that bags or other automatic restraints be installed in all new cars by 1984. If people would wear their belts, more than 10,000 lives could be saved a year; since they will not, the government will make them be safe despite themselves. Many object to this loss of freedom or to the increased selling price of cars, but clearly traffic safety is a social concern. Saving lives will also save money, money spent for insurance, hospitals, and funerals.

Even before the appearance of the safety issue, investigators came to realize that most, or much of Los Angeles' air pollution came from exhaust emissions. Since the car makers would not voluntarily install control devices, the State of California passed a law requiring that all 1962 models be so equipped. The federal government in 1965 enacted a similar law for the whole nation to take effect in 1967. In the ten years since, federal emission control standards have been gradually intensified, despite the continuing protest of the industry that it could not meet more rigid requirements. Recently the decreased fuel economy of the 1973 models combined with the beginning of the oil crisis gave Detroit a new argument to use, and the standards have been relaxed. The industry's complaints have some justification; control of pollutants is difficult. The catalytic converter is not the answer, for it is expensive and tends to produce sulphuric acid fumes. Researchers are working on new types of engines, for example, the stratified-charge motor developed by Honda, a Japanese firm, and are also re-examining the diesel, an engine which can meet most of the original, stringent requirements. Olds is offering a diesel engine as an option for 1978. Because of growing concern over economy and the rapidly rising price of cars, much of the force has disappeared from the movement to eliminate auto pollution, but the pollution remains. As the public has proved time and time again, it will tolerate almost any inconvenience and even danger involved with car ownership. Personal mobility is more important than the harmful social consequences of the car.

In the early 1970s a problem foreseen only by a few experts began to appear: Oil shortages and increased petroleum prices, which began to go up early in 1973. By summer a gasoline shortage had developed. Ten thousand service stations went out of business that year, and the surviving stations were forced to limit sales to five or ten gallons a car and to close on Sunday. Many suspected that the big oil companies had contrived to create the shortage to increase profits, and the Federal Trade Commission charged that the companies had used illegal, monopolistic methods to reduce sales to independent wholesalers and retailers. The fuel crisis escalated when the Moslem nations used a limited oil embargo after the October, 1973, middle eastern war to try to force the United States to cut its support for Israel. The price of middle eastern oil rose from $2.59 a barrel late in 1972 to $10.80 in January, 1974. The increase resulted in further inflation of the cost of gasoline. From 1972 to 1974, the price per gallon rose from thirty-forty cents to fifty-sixty cents. To force decreased consumption, the government established a 55 mph speed limit but could do little more. The impact on the American economy was disastrous, especially since it was already in a period of recession. Oil is the most vital single commodity to an industrial nation. Detroit could not respond, and decreasing car sales forced massive layoffs. Prices of almost every product went up. Inflation and recession were uncontrollable.

The worst of the oil crisis had passed by the end of 1974, but the price of gasoline did not come down, and neither did the price of most other goods. Clearly there is no easy solution to the oil problem, for the United States imports an increasing amount of petroleum in spite of government attempts to limit consumption. Domestic reserves are inadequate to meet domestic demands. Despite the obvious, Congress has delayed creating a systematic energy program which will increase domestic production of energy and gradually reduce American dependence on foreign oil. There is no shortage currently, but the problem will not disappear. Not just the car is involved; heating, electricity, industrial production, our whole way of life are at stake, and the future is dark. There is not much oil left in the world.

The oil crisis resulted for a while in increased sales of small, mostly imported cars, but Americans have recently shown that they still prefer big ones. They also refuse to obey the 55 mph speed limit, which unexpectedly cut death rates on the highway. Most Americans complain but still pay the sixty-seventy cents a gallon that gasoline now costs, and they have slowed down a little but still drive about as much as before. Consequently, the government has begun to impose economy standards, which will gradually increase in the 1980s. We can no longer afford to have cars that average twelve-fourteen miles per gallon; that average must be doubled, and the government will ensure that it is.

To gauge the many effects of the car, look around, read a book, or go to a movie. Its impact is everywhere. Novelists make cars their subjects. Already mentioned is Steinbeck's *The Grapes of Wrath*, but there are many others: James Agee's *A Death in the Family* (1967) or Jack Karouac's *On The Road* (1957) or William Faulkner's *The Reivers* (1962). Poets, painters, and sculptors have also immortalized the car. One of the most interesting works is Edward Kienholz's tableau "Back Seat Dodge '38" (1964), an actual telescoped car with a plaster couple making out on the rear seat; certain museums discreetly closed the door before allowing the public admittance. Movies would hardly exist without cars. The Keystone Cops, Laurel and Hardy, and many other famous actors have used them as comedy props. And cars can create an excitement that few actors can approach; for proof see *Bonnie and Clyde* or most James Bond films. The Disney Studios have even anthropomorphized a car in several films about Herbie, the invincible VW. For many, real automobiles are examples of hollow, rolling sculpture. Some, the affluent, collect and display examples of the most beautiful, and others, also affluent, customize their vans into gaudy mobile bedrooms. Architects have to consider the car when planning shopping centers, hotels, and office buildings. Many follow motor racing, and the Indianapolis 500 is an American folk festival. Even in the wilderness one cannot escape the camper, the all-terrain vehicle, or the trail bike. The motor vehicle is American life.

The impact of the car has become so pervasive, that some of its critics maintain that it has become America's worst domestic enemy. Obviously with the decreasing reserves of oil, there will be substantial changes in everyday life in the immediate future, but the car, or some kind of motor vehicle, will long remain part of America life. The development of cities during the last fifty years has revolved around the motor vehicle. We cannot now rebuild our cities around some other kind of transportation, because the social and financial costs would be prohibitive. Yet mass transportation will become more and more necessary as the years pass. The only possible answer is a combination of motor and rail travel. Buses will take passengers to rail terminals or directly to work, and the private car will decrease in importance. Automobiles will remain in use, becoming progressively smaller and lighter to conserve petroleum. No doubt people will continue to use them for pleasure, but they will be an increasingly more expensive luxury. It is doubtful that any electric or steam engine will supplant internal combustion. Electrics are not practical, for they are too slow and too short-ranged; and steamers suffer severe technical problems. The gasoline engine will likely give way to the diesel, which is more economical and longer lived. Historians, however, should be careful in making predictions, although the above seem safe, at least for the foreseeable future. The car culture will survive in some form, but the rest is speculation.

SUGGESTED READINGS

For general treatments of the car, see John B. Rae's *The Road and the Car in American Life* (1971), James J. Flink's *America Adopts the Automobile* (1970), and Flink's historical critique *The Car Culture* (1975). A well-illustrated account is Stephen W. Sears' *The American Heritage History of the Automobile in America* (1977).

Two works on highways are Jean Labatut and Wheaton J. Lane, editors, *Highways in Our Life: A Symposium* (1950, reprint, 1972) and Richard O. Davies, editor, *The Age of Asphalt: The Automobile, the Freeway, and the Condition of Metropolitan America* (1975).

Books on urban America include Norman T. Moline's *Mobility and the Small Town, 1900-1930: Transportation Change in Oregon, Illinois* (1971), William H. Wilson's *Coming of Age: Urban America, 1915-1945* (1974), and Robert A. Caro's vituperative biography *The Power Broker: Robert Moses and the Fall of New York* (1974).

John B. Rae's *The American Automobile: A Brief History* (1965) surveys the industry. See also Lawrence J. White's *The Automobile Industry Since 1945* (1971), David L. Lewis' *The Public Image of Henry Ford: An American Folk Hero and His Company* (1976), and Automobile Quarterly's *The American Automobile Since 1775* (1971).

Two other studies are Reynold M. Wik's *Henry Ford and Grass-roots America* (1972) about the farm and Cynthia G. Dettelbach's *In the Driver's Seat: The Automobile in American Literature and Popular Culture* (1976).

The two most famous critics of the car are Wilfred Owen and Lewis Mumford, both of whom have written many books. A representative volume by Owen is *The Accessible City* (1972) and one by Mumford is *The Urban Prospect* (1968). The best recent polemic is Kenneth Schneider's *Autokind vs. Mankind* (1971).

CHAPTER TWO

The Growth of Corporate America

DALE ROYALTY

In December, 1901, a few months after assuming office, President Theodore Roosevelt told Congress that

> the tremendous and highly complex industrial development which went on with ever accelerated rapidity during the latter half of the nineteenth century brings us face to face, at the beginning of the twentieth, with very serious social problems.

Industrial development had created problems in America. Between 1873 and 1901 the economy had suffered two recessions and two major depressions and the resulting hard times had generated considerable social upheaval and violence. From the great strike of 1877 to the Pullman strike of 1894, labor and capital carried on what amounted to war. Some workers and intellectuals were attracted to socialism, communism, and anarchism. Farmers felt themselves increasingly isolated from industrial and urban America and were restive under what they believed to be a capitalist conspiracy to hold rural areas of the nation under their control. Businessmen also felt the disruption of the boom and bust, since intense competition during the boom periods led to waste, inefficiency, and overcapitalization culminating in bankruptcy during the bust. Political institutions seemed powerless to hold special interests accountable to the public welfare.

Even as Roosevelt spoke to Congress about the problems of industrialization, a revolution in the nature of American capitalism was well under way. This revolution rejected the individualistic, market place ideal sought by reformers during the Jacksonian era and substituted for it a vision of a nationally integrated, interdependent society founded on a community of property interest.

Recognizing that the boom and bust cycle was disrupting orderly business growth and creating serious challenges to the American social system based on private property, such businessmen as J. P. Morgan had begun a campaign to bring the market place economy under control by consolidating competing businesses into large corporations that could control the market rather than be controlled by it. The depressions of the era spurred the consolidation movement by weeding out weaker companies and encouraging the survivors to combine. In the years following the major depression of the 1890s, the trend toward consolidation became a rush as five thousand companies were merged into three hundred new corporations or trusts. The culmination of the consolidation movement came in March, 1901, nine months before Roosevelt's message, when Morgan created the United States Steel Company. Capitalized at over a billion dollars, U.S. Steel was by far the largest corporation of its day and controlled 62 percent of the industry. Other, smaller companies, controlled even larger shares of their markets. American Telephone and Telegraph, founded in 1894, controlled all telephone communication in the nation; Standard Oil controlled 90 percent of the oil industry in 1899; and International Harvester Company dominated 85 percent of the farm implement business in 1902. Although monopoly was never achieved in any industry and the control of the largest companies declined during the twentieth century, consolidation did limit the cutthroat competition characteristic of the nineteenth century. The price of steel rails, for example, remained at $28 per ton for fifteen years after the formation of U.S. Steel despite large swings in production costs.

As hard times advanced the trend toward consolidation in business, they contributed to unrest and increasing radicalism among workers. Because much of the capital necessary to create the industrial base was acquired by keeping production costs as low as possible, workers drew low wages and put in long hours in poor working conditions. The average industrial worker made from $.14 to $.20 per hour over a sixty hour week. His working conditions were such that in the first years of the twentieth century nearly 25,000 workers were killed and over 100,000 seriously injured each year. Living conditions for American workers, bad in the best of times, became intolerable during depressions. In these circumstances, labor unions developed and grew. Spontaneous strikes and attacks on company property, which had been common earlier, evolved by the late 1870s into the permanent union. Between 1871 and 1885, the Knights of Labor grew from 50,000 members to 700,000. Rejecting the market place concept in labor, workers were attempting to gain control of their lives and work through collective action.

Farmers, too, were in trouble. Prices for agricultural commodities declined steadily from the Civil War to 1896, leaving farmers in debt for the farm machinery and land necessary to increase production in an attempt to maintain income. More and more they found themselves dependent on an industrial-financial complex they neither understood nor were able to influence. The mid-western farm centers, like the worker communities of northeastern cities, were hot-beds of discontent and agitation during the late nineteenth century. Farmers, like workers, began to see the solution to their problems in collective action. Such organizations as the Grange, the Wheel, and the Farmer's Alliances had a significant political impact in farm belt states from the 1870s through the 1890s. The demands of farmers were three-fold: inflation of the currency, public regulation of vital industries such as railroads, and expansion of foreign markets for agricultural goods.

Farmers, workers, and businessmen alike were rejecting laissez-faire individualistic capitalism in favor of consolidation and collective action to solve the serious problems created by industrialization. But despite the similarity of form their methods took, each group thought the solution to its particular problems lay in controlling or suppressing the others. Conflict between them smoldered and reached a crisis during the severe depression which began in 1893. Political parties such as the Populists and Socialists emerged to call for restrictions on private property; large corporations began a concerted effort to destroy labor unions; anarchists began a campaign of violence directed at business and political leaders.

American society seemed on the brink of tearing itself apart. If republican political principles and private property were to survive into the twentieth century, reform was essential. This was the conclusion reached by business leaders such as J. P. Morgan, Mark Hanna, and Brooks Adams; political leaders like Theodore Roosevelt and John Hay; and such social critics and intellectuals as Frederick Jackson Turner, Henry Adams, and Alfred T. Mahan.

The thoughts of James Madison over a century before were a guide to understanding the crisis of the 1890s. In his remarks during the Constitutional Convention and in Federalist Paper #10, Madison had concluded that republican political principles and the right of private property could only be established where a community of interest existed between those with and those without property. In his article, "The Significance of the Frontier in American History," published in 1893, Frederick Jackson Turner followed a similar line of thought when he argued that the frontier provided the community of interest necessary for social stability by creating the opportunity to acquire property. From Jamestown to California, territorial expansion had muted conflict that might have otherwise arisen from the inequitable distribution of property. But the census of 1890 reported that a frontier no longer existed in America and, as Turner concluded, forebode ill for the community of interest-based property rights.

Based on this analysis of the American experience, a solution to the crisis of the 1890s lay in recreating the community of interest in property and expansion of opportunity. The first step was to recognize the legitimacy of consolidation, whether farmer, laborer, or businessman, and to reject hostility between these groups in favor of cooperation. A beginning seemed to emerge in 1896 when business leaders Morgan and Hanna as well as labor leaders like Samuel Gompers and many in the farm belt rejected William Jennings Bryan's call for a return to individualistic laissez-faire capitalism and supported William McKinley for president. The same sentiment of cooperation was voiced by Teddy Roosevelt in 1902 when he said:

> This is an era of federation and combination. Exactly as businessmen find they must often work through corporations, and as it is a constant tendency of these corporations to grow larger, so it is often necessary for laboring men to work in federations, and these have become important factors of modern industrial life.

The second step in solving the crisis was to renew economic growth. The crisis of the 1890s was interpreted as the result of a slowed growth rate when the industrial plant had expanded beyond the capacity of the American market to consume its product. The solution, as seen by men like William McKinley, John D. Rockefeller, Theodore Roosevelt, Alfred T. Mahan, Brooks Adams, and Frank Vanderlip, was renewed growth through expansion of foreign markets. Between 1898 and 1917 the United States joined the scramble among western nations for overseas colonies and foreign economic preferences by fighting wars in Cuba, the Philippines, and China; acquiring as colonies the Philippines, Puerto Rico, Guam, the Virgin Islands, and part of the Samoan islands; annexing Hawaii; and establishing economic and military control of Cuba, Haiti, Santo Domingo, Panama, and Nicaragua. The famous Open Door notes calling for equal access to China among trading nations were issued in 1899 and 1900 by Secretary of State John Hay. It was clear that the Open Door policy applied equally to the whole world. As President McKinley said in his last public address in 1901:

> Our capacity to produce has developed so enormously and our products have so multiplied that the problem of more markets requires our urgent and immediate attention. What we produce beyond our domestic consumption must have a foreign outlet and we should sell everywhere we can, and buy wherever the buying will enlarge our sales and productions, and thereby make a greater demand for home labor.

Thus the revolution, largely achieved by the time Roosevelt addressed Congress in 1901, rejected the Jacksonian ideal of liberal capitalism based on individualism and the free operation of the market place. In its place was emerging a much more interdependent social system, a corporate state, based on cooperation among special interest groups whose common goals were to maintain a community of property interest and to further economic opportunity through growth.

When Teddy Roosevelt succeeded to the presidency, he followed a policy designed to use the power of the federal government to institutionalize and stabilize the new socioeconomic order and to insure the principle of accountability to the general welfare. Under the progressive administrations of Roosevelt, William H. Taft, and Woodrow Wilson, the federal government took an ever-increasing role in regulating private capital. Regulation was considered to be in the public interest, but it was also in the interest of the community of property interest. As big businessmen came to realize and, after initial hostility, began to support, regulation encouraged the stability of property.

The dedication to growth through foreign expansion was continued by both Republican and Democratic administrations during the progressive period. Roosevelt's high-handed actions in Panama, Santo Domingo, and Cuba were based on the policy of expanding United States foreign trade opportunities. He made this aspect of his foreign policy clear in his 1903 message to Congress in support of a new treaty with Cuba:

> [the treaty] is demanded on considerations of broad national policy as well as by our economic interest. It will do harm to no industry. It will benefit many industries. It is in the interest of our people . . . because it intimately concerns us to develop and secure the rich Cuban market for our farmers, artisans, merchants, and manufacturers.

Wilson, despite his campaign attack on "dollar diplomacy," also supported the policy of growth through foreign expansion. In his speech accepting the Democratic party nomination for President, Wilson declared:

> Our industries have expanded to such a point that they will burst their jackets if they cannot find a free outlet to the markets of the world. . . . Our domestic markets no longer suffice. We need foreign markets.

That commitment to foreign trade expansion was carried out by the Underwood-Simmons tariff, which generally reduced rates; by his vigorous defense of United States Caribbean interests in Haiti, Nicaragua, and Mexico; and by his pro-business neutrality policy between 1914 and 1917. By the end of World War I the United States had become the dominant economic factor in the world and New York had replaced London as the world's financial capital.

During the 1920s Republican economic policy, formulated by Secretary of the Treasury Andrew Mellon and Secretary of Commerce Herbert Hoover, heavily favored the corporate state by eliminating or reducing taxes on great wealth and on corporations and by pursuing domestic policies favorable to business. But at the same time a shortsighted high tariff policy cut deeply into the ability of American industry to find markets for its products abroad. The slack in foreign trade was more than taken up, however, by the development of consumerism at home. High wages in industry, led by Henry Ford's pioneering five dollars a day, coupled with consumer credit, high-pressure advertising, and assembly line production, stimulated a new expansive industry in such personal consumer goods as the automobile, refrigerators, radios, and electrical applicances. Maintenance of consumer demand in America became at least as important as an expanding overseas market to the growth still considered essential for prosperity and social stability.

It was the failure to maintain the pace of consumer demand at the same rate that productive capacity was growing that was the fundamental weakness of the economy of the twenties. With the economy weighted on the investment side, speculation in stocks, bonds, and real estate boomed while investment in new plants and equipment began to fall after 1926. When the bubble of speculation burst in 1929, the whole economy tumbled down in 1930 and 1931.

The New Deal in Franklin Roosevelt's first term was an effort to revive the corporate state under government sponsorship. The National Industrial Recovery Act of 1933 suspended anti-trust laws and companies were urged to combine under codes intended to raise prices by agreement. Labor combination was aided by section 7A of the act, which gave government protection to union efforts to organize industry. The unemployed were temporarily aided through the public works section of the law. Farmers were organized by the Agricultural Adjustment Act of 1933 to cut production and raise prices.

By 1936, however, the New Deal "brain trust" had abandoned the concept of government supervised combination in favor of pump-priming, or in economic terms — compensatory spending. Compensatory spending by government could encourage growth by providing the economic stimulus lacking from either consumer or investment sectors of the economy.

By the middle of his second term, with his domestic programs under attack by southern Democrats as well as Republicans and with the depression still serious, Roosevelt began to lean toward the view of Secretary of State Cordell Hull that American prosperity could be restored and maintained only by reviving the international trade system that had collapsed in 1929. In short, Roosevelt was beginning to accept the notion that the Open Door world was essential to American economic growth and social stability.

When war broke out in Asia in 1937 and in Europe in 1939, Roosevelt became increasingly concerned about the economic, political, and military consequences of a world dominated by Axis Powers. By 1940, with Europe controlled by Hitler and Asia by Japan, he was convinced that America had a vital stake in the outcome of the fighting. In a December 1940 fireside chat he warned that, in the event of an Axis victory, all Americans would be living at the point of a gun loaded with economic as well as military bullets. Thus in 1941 the United States unofficially entered the war in the Atlantic in order to bolster the fading prospects of the Allies and began clandestine aid to the Asian enemies of Japan. After Pearl Harbor the federal government and business forged an economic partnership that made the United States the "Arsenal of Democracy" and in the process quickly ended the lingering effects of the depression.

At the end of the war, American policymakers were determined that peace would not mean depression and embarked on a policy to establish the Open Door world. In 1945 and 1946 State Department spokesmen undertook a public campaign to prepare the American people for continued international commitments. On November 22, 1945, before the annual meeting of the National Council for the Social Studies, Clair Wilcox, Director of the State Department's Office of International Trade Policy, set the tone for this campaign when he urged an aggressive commitment to world power:

> The political and the economic structure of the world has been shaken by war. It is obvious to everyone today that international relationships in industry, finance, and commerce must be rebuilt. The opportunity for making major alterations in this structure is now at hand. But time is short. Our power as social architects is greater this year and next than it will be a few years hence. If we delay until the international economy has hardened into a new mold, our greatest opportunity to shape it in the patterns of peace and prosperity will have been lost. The time for decision is now.

A year later in 1946 Under Secretary of State for Economic Affairs, William C. Clayton, explained to the Foreign Trade Convention that:

the objective of the foreign economic policy of the United States Government is to lay the foundation for peace by an expansion in world economy, that is, by an increase in the production, distribution, and consumption of goods through out the world.

Pursuit of the Open Door in the era following World War II, however, was a difficult and dangerous undertaking. Two world wars in a single generation had left European societies exhausted and their economies broken. In Asia, in the Middle East, and in Africa, colonial nations were overthrowing European control and seeking self-determination. In this chaotic and revolutionary world the United States had committed itself to preserving the status quo. During the Truman administration the United States embarked on an unprecedented peacetime program of foreign military and economic aid: to Europe through the Marshall plan and the North Atlantic Treaty Organization; to Japan through the military occupation administered by Douglas MacArthur; to South Korea in money, arms, and soldiers; to nationalist China ruled by Chiang Kai-shek in military aid; to France in financial support for their effort to reestablish colonial control in Indochina; to dictatorial regimes in Greece and Turkey through economic and military grants; and to Israel in military, political, and economic support. At home, too, the Open Door policy resulted in unprecedented spending for defense and weapons technology.

In the years following, the United States has not only protected the access of corporations to raw materials in foreign countries and their foreign investments, but has also guaranteed with social security, welfare, and minimum wage legislation a high level of buying power in the American market. In addition, the federal government has contributed directly to the success of American corporations by purchasing their products, especially in the aerospace and defense industries; granting such tax preferences as the oil depletion allowance; and guaranteeing loans to faltering companies, as in the case of the Lockheed Company in 1971.

The Pax Americana has been good for business in America and in the industrial nations allied with the United States. Under the protection of American military and political power, business in America, Europe, and Japan has enjoyed a quarter-century of phenomenal growth and the material wealth of the population of industrial nations has never been greater. Today such private corporations as General Motors, International Telephone and Telegraph, International Business Machines, Volkswagen, Royal Dutch Shell, Exxon, British Petroleum, British Leyland, Mitsubishi, and Sears span the globe with their factories and products. These multinational conglomerates of economic power are the culmination of the vision of stability, growth, and community of interest advanced by the reformers of the early twentieth century and variously interpreted and modified over the years.

But today, following the tragedy of our Vietnam experience, the ability and willingness of the United States to continue the pursuit of the Open Door world is doubtful. A new instability in international affairs has complicated the pursuit of profit. Many third world countries have recognized the power to bring the industrial world to its knees by withholding such vital raw materials as oil (Arabia), bauxite (Jamaica), or copper (Chile). At the same time, the multinational corporation no longer depends solely on the United States to protect its interests or encourage a favorable international business environment. As John Gallagher, in charge of Sears' international operations, told an assembly of businessmen in December 1971:

> As far as the protection of U.S. private investment in Latin America goes, we in the business community are literally on our own. . . . If we are on our own, as I think we are, then we must also act on our own.

The leaders of the multinational corporations believe the future of the world lies with them rather than with the outdated and ineffectual nation-state. Raising the national vision of J. P. Morgan and Teddy Roosevelt to global level, they see a world without national borders and without ideologies, a world benignly organized by the corporation to the end of prosperity and consumerism — the global shopping center.

The multinational is without doubt the most powerful new force in the world today. But it has emerged at the same time that significant movements in societies across the world have begun to question the validity of profit and material growth as the goal of mankind.

Many serious and concerned scientists are questioning whether the earth's eco-system can survive another century of industrial growth on the scale of the past century. People are asking what point there is to an ever-increasing supply of goods and services when that kind of growth may mean a catastrophic deterioration of the environment. Will we all die surrounded by a multitude of products designed to cater to creature comforts and convenience? Many people are also questioning the quality of their lives locked into jobs that seem to have no purpose other than more production. Both the concern over the environment and the quality of life are basic attacks on the assumptions sustaining the multination corporations and the vision of the world as a global shopping center.

Underlying these serious concerns is a purely practical one, the recognition of the dwindling supply of key natural resources necessary for continued industrial growth. In the economy of scarcity that we are now entering, the problem of the 1890s, property versus personal rights, will again emerge: *who* will get *what* is left? As the giant multinationals continue to increase their hold on the earth's resources, growing demands for government action to control and equitably distribute resources will be likely. Such government action, however, is unwanted by the new global corporations. They would prefer the demise of the nation-state, to be replaced by the corporation as a more efficient, albeit less democratic, means of allocating the world's resources.

What will happen when governments and corporations clash? The outcome is uncertain. There will be struggle, that much is clear.

SUGGESTED READINGS

Barnet, Richard J., & Ronald E. Muller, *Global Reach, The Power of the Multinational Corporations*, 1974.

Chandler, Alfred D., *Strategy and Structure*, 1962.

Garraty, John A., *The New Commonwealth*, 1968.

Heilbroner, Robert L., *The Economic Transformation of America*, 1977.

Kindleberger, Charles P., *The World in Depression*, 1970.

Kolko, Gabriel, *Main Currents in Modern American History*, 1976.

Leuchtenburg, William, *The Perils of Prosperity*, 1958.

Freidel, Frank, *Franklin Roosevelt and the New Deal*, 1963.

Wiebe, R. H., *The Search for Order*, 1967.

Williams, William A., *The Tragedy of American Diplomacy*, 1972.

Reflecting Freudian influences, The Cry (1893), by Norwegian expressionist Edward Munch, depicts subconscious and irrational fears of the unknown. (National Gallery of Art)

CHAPTER THREE

Themes in American Social and Intellectual History

JOHN W. STOREY

American society has undergone vast changes in the twentieth century. Rural villages have given way to metropolises; family-owned enterprises have succumbed to multinational corporations. And in the realm of thought, the intellectual certainty of the nineteenth century has been steadily eroded. As the eminent philosopher-journalist, Walter Lippmann, observed, "our ancestors knew their way from birth through death into eternity, but we are puzzled about [the] day after tomorrow." These alterations in society and thought have affected all Americans, but have they also produced the estrangement or conformity detected by some contemporary social critics? Are Americans today moving toward a mass society of anonymous beings?

In the early nineteenth century American society and thought were characterized by a simplicity and certainty which today appear quaint. Society in the first half of the nineteenth century revolved around small communities in which individuals generally knew one another. Associations and contacts were personal. Except for a few sizeable cities along the Atlantic seaboard and the interior waterways, scattered farms and villages dominated the landscape. In 1860 not quite 20 percent of the population lived in urban areas of 2,500 or more. And despite the mobility of the population, families frequently remained in the same vicinity, producing extended units of parents, grandparents, aunts, uncles, and cousins. This contributed to a sense of security, both psychological and material. Aside from the family, the most important institution was the church, which furnished the community with steady guideposts based upon moral absolutes. Significantly, secular thought in the early nineteenth century reinforced the belief in absolute laws. The natural and social sciences were in harmony. Newtonian physics postulated an orderly, mechanistic universe governed by natural laws, and social theorists assumed that similar laws discoverable through reason underlay human affairs. Whether in economics, politics, or religion, free and responsible individuals presumably could perceive the universal laws behind human events. This, along with the steady westward march of American settlers, contributed to an optimistic belief in progress. By the beginning of the twentieth century this idyllic picture was fading. Enormous economic and urban changes after the Civil War reduced the significance of individuals, while developments in the natural and social sciences challenged intellectual absolutism and created doubts about the rationality of mankind. Twentieth century Americans were losing their moorings. "Never were roads wilder," as Lippmann put it, "nor sign posts fewer."

Rapid industrialization and urbanization wrought vast social alterations in the latter nineteenth century. Corporations, organized by groups of people to carry out specific enterprises, increasingly displaced individuals as the most important units in the economy. Individual enterpreneurs could no more easily compete with large corporations than solitary laborers could bargain for better wages and hours. Collective bargaining through unionization was thus a normal and, for labor, essential outgrowth of the organization of business. American farmers likewise discovered the necessity of organization as prices of basic staples — cotton, corn, and wheat — steadily declined in the post-Appomattox years. Although family-operated units continued to be the rule, farmers increasingly joined organizations like the Grange of the 1870s, the Alliances of the 1880s, and the bureaus of the early twentieth century, in an effort to alleviate economic problems. Business leaders, meanwhile, disseminated their views through manufacturers' associations and chambers of commerce. So by the twentieth century organized units were rapidly replacing individuals in all sectors of the economy — business, labor, and agriculture. The rugged individual, previously the hallmark of society, now found his niche in and made his contribution through one or more of the various groups.

Urbanization, which accelerated after the Civil War, had a similar impact. In 1860 there were only nine cities in the United States with a population of 100,000 or more; there were fifty by 1910. While certain areas, such as the mid-Atlantic and New England states, were more heavily urbanized than others, all sections of the nation experienced steady urban growth. By 1910 the total urban population was almost 46 percent, and by 1920 urbanites constituted a majority (51.2 percent) of the American populace. Paradoxically, as people from the American and European countrysides gathered in close proximity in the city, they frequently experienced social isolation. The personal, face-to-face contacts enjoyed by residents of small, rural communities were lost in the impersonal crowds of the city. Moreover, the extended family, which had previously afforded a sense of security, was replaced by the nuclear family, consisting of husband, wife, and children. The phenomenon of individual loneliness amid urban throngs contributed to the emergence of clubs, fraternities, brotherhoods, and youthful gangs. And shrewd urban political bosses quickly recognized that they could extend their power base from poor immigrants to the more affluent middle classes by providing social and recreational activities which relieved the anonymity of city life. Like industrialization, then, urbanization compelled individuals to forge organizations in order to find meaning and exert influence.

The alterations in society affecting the individual were paralleled by major developments in the natural and social sciences. Specifically, the certainty so characteristic of nineteenth century thought was undermined. Newtonian physics, which had long provided a scientific basis for social theories resting on immutable natural laws, was toppled from its pedestal by the twentieth century quantum physics of Max Planck, Albert Einstein, and Niels Bohr. Probability and relativity thereafter replaced the laws of causality and determinism. The orderly and mechanistic world of Newton was out of place in the relativistic universe of Einstein.

This development in science was paralleled by an expression

of philosophical relativity — pragmatism, one of the few original contributions by Americans to intellectual history. As enunciated by William James and John Dewey, pragmatism was a refutation of the Social Darwinian views of Herbert Spencer and William Graham Sumner. Specifically, the pragmatists denied that the universe behaved in accordance with unchanging, deterministic natural laws, an assumption basic to Social Darwinism. Instead, James and Dewey insisted that the universe was in a perpetual state of unpredictable flux and change, the outcome of which was unforeseeable.

Despite the espousal of relativity, pragmatism was optimistic. Inasmuch as it stressed man's ability to influence the environment, however slightly, through reason, experimentation, and willpower, pragmatism was not only in harmony with the generally optimistic mood of Americans, but also furnished a rationale for those reformers of the late nineteenth and early twentieth centuries who wanted to curb the trusts, clean up the cities, expand the regulatory functions of government, and assist the downtrodden. But how could reformers be sure of the desirability of their objectives? Pragmatism offered a solution, for it was also a method for determining truth in a relativistic world. To be sure, truth itself was relative, continually changing as circumstances changed. Nevertheless, James and Dewey assumed that the truthfulness of an idea could be determined by its consequences. That is, if an idea produced socially beneficial results, it was truth for that place and time.

The discovery of truth, moreover, need not be a haphazard, trial-and-error process. Somewhat like the natural scientists, the pragmatists, especially Dewey, maintained that an hypothesis could be articulated and tested, its consequences assessed, and its truthfulness thereby determined. Although error could never be completely eliminated, it could be minimized by redefining and testing hypotheses. Significantly, Dewey the reformer was critical of the New Deal because it impressed him as chaotic rather than scientific experimentation. In a world of uncertainty, where everything was continually shifting, some order could still be achieved by constantly thinking and experimenting. James and Dewey confidently assumed that the flow of history, to some degree, would yield to creative intelligence.

While the pragmatists were dismantling philosophical absolutism, thinkers in other disciplines similarly assailed rigidity.

All these men were not necessarily pragmatists, but like the pragmatists they all stressed the need for change as a result of alterations in society. A University of Wisconsin sociologist, Edward A. Ross, *Sin and Society* (1907), argued that moral standards suitable in the simple, agrarian society of Thomas Jefferson were often unsuitable in the more complex urban, industrial society of Theodore Roosevelt. Sin, which Ross defined as any activity by one or more persons injurious to other people, was personal in a simple society characterized by face-to-face relationships. Responsibility for misdeeds could therefore be rather easily determined, and presumably those responsible would experience some sense of guilt. But in a world of corporations, where distant boards of directors managed affairs for stockholders, sin had become impersonal. Dangerous foods, drugs, and other merchandise could be foisted upon the public without any of the groups involved in the industrial process — manufacturers, wholesalers, retailers, advertisers, and corporation directors — feeling any sense of guilt or responsibility. New ethical codes, thought Ross, were thus needed to hold impersonal corporations accountable.

Within the legal profession, long a bastion of absolutism, similar trends were evident. While Supreme Court Justice Oliver Wendell Holmes, Jr., doubted that law was an absolute standard against which the affairs of government could be measured, later legal scholars, known as legal realists, candidly insisted that law was relative, generally being fashioned and refashioned through judicial interpretation. Indeed, many legal realists assumed that it was the responsibility of judges to keep law relevant through interpretation.

Meanwhile, Herbert Croly, *The Promise of American Life* (1909), an editor of *The New Republic* magazine and a perennial student at Harvard, suggested the usage of Hamiltonian means (strong government) to achieve Jeffersonian ends (individual liberty and freedom). Whereas Jefferson had feared centralized government, believing it a threat to liberty and freedom, Croly maintained that strong government was now essential to protect individual liberty and freedom against further encroachments by economic monopolies. Government had to be strong, Croly believed, to control corporations in the public interest. And historian Charles A. Beard, *An Economic Interpretation of the Constitution of the United States* (1913), a major figure among the new school of socio-economic historians, contended that the Constitution, instead of being the embodiment of absolute law, was an economically inspired document drafted in response to conditions of the 1780s. By implication, the Constitution should be adjusted so as to allow government to deal with the new economic and political realities of the twentieth century.

Religious thought likewise reflected the impact of the urban, industrial, and intellectual shifts of the late nineteenth and early twentieth centuries. Evangelical Protestantism had traditionally emphasized individual salvation. But in the industrial and urban climate of the late nineteenth century, numerous ministers believed the church should also address itself to social ills — slums, inadequate wages and unsafe working conditions, corporate and political abuses, and child labor. The outgrowth of this concern was the social gospel, whose leading spokesman in the early twentieth century was Walter Rauschenbusch, a northern Baptist who had pastored a small congregation in the Hell's Kitchen area of New York city before joining the faculty at Rochester Theological Seminary. In *Christianity and the Social Crisis* (1906), *For God and the People* (1909), *Christianizing the Social Order* (1912), and *A Theology for the Social Gospel* (1917), Rauschenbusch supported a social application of Christian teachings, diagnosed social injustices, and maintained a middle-ground between theological liberals and conservatives. Whereas liberals de-emphasized sin and were overly optimistic about human progress, conservatives stressed Original Sin and remained skeptical of human improvement. Rauschenbusch assailed liberals for attempting to explain sin away in environmental terms, while rebuking conservatives for failing to perceive sin in a social context.

Although the social gospel was more evident in the North where the problems of industrialization and urbanization were more acute, it nevertheless made inroads in the more rural and theologically conservative South. Illiteracy, farm tenancy, racial discrimination, and labor ills in the tobacco, textile, lumber, and mineral industries of the South aroused the social consciousness of many southern ministers. A Mississippi Baptist minister, Charles H. Otken, *The Ills of the South* (1894), condemned the crop-lien system; the rector of St. John's Episcopal Church in Montgomery, Alabama, Edgar Gardner

Murphy, opposed child labor and supported better education and racial justice; a North Carolina Presbyterian, Alexander J. McKelway, labored in behalf of age-and-hour laws; and a Texas Baptist clergyman, Joseph M. Dawson, called for racial justice and a social application of Christian ideals. So southern Protestantism, too, felt the impact of socially conscious ministers who desired change.

Intellectual developments such as these made for a rather optimistic mood in the early twentieth century. To be sure, rapid industrialization and urbanization had spawned staggering problems. But reformers and thinkers, freed from the absolutist dogmas of the past by quantum physics and the philosophy of pragmatism, were confident of the future. The break with the past was accentuated by the ready usage of "new" to proclaim the New Republic, the New Democracy, the New Woman, the New History, the New Freedom, and New Nationalism, the New Education, and the New Psychology. As Walter Lord noticed, these were "the good years." However onerous, problems were assumed to be within man's ability to resolve. But was man rational? Investigations along other lines not only raised serious doubts, but also foreshadowed the grave new world of *1984.*

Studies by Sigmund Freud, an Austrian psychologist, and Ivan Pavlov, a Russian physiologist, enormously influenced popular ideas about human nature. Freudian psychologists saw man as a creature driven by blind impulses originating in the unconscious and shaped by childhood experiences, sex drives, and inhibitions, while Pavlov and the behavioral psychologists described man as something of an automaton whose behavior consisted of conditioned reflexes to stimuli. In either case, man was stripped of free will. Behavior was a matter of impulses or stimuli. And both interpretations, so many observers feared, seemingly provided scientific justification for disregarding traditional conventions and morals.

These theories of human behavior had particularly serious implications for democratic thought. Democracy rested upon the assumption that individual voters, guided by reason and a free discussion of issues, would arrive at intelligent decisions. But in view of new insights into human nature, how valid was this popular assumption? In the summer of 1912 the twenty-three-year-old Walter Lippmann, one of the original trio of editors of *The New Republic*, journeyed to the Maine woods to write a book reconciling Freudian psychology and democratic politics. The result was *A Preface to Politics* (1913).

Lippmann maintained that politicans of the past had always governed by "taboo." That is, they had made laws for what people ought not to do, thereby inducing large scale neuroses. Prohibitory, or repressive, legislation, such as the Sherman Anti-Trust Act, aroused all the social evil, argued Lippmann, that Freud discovered in individual psychology. The hope of the future, the youthful journalist thought, lay in "sublimation" — that is, the direction of society's impulses toward desirable ends. This called for extraordinary statesmanship, for irrational impulses were stronger than reason. Thus Nietzschean-like statesmen seeking support for socially desirable programs would be justified in couching their objectives in terms of some "myth" which would elicit mass enthusiasm, rather than explaining their goals in honest and rational language. Such questionable methods could be excused because of the desirability of the goal. In attempting to graft Freudian theories onto democratic politics, the young journalist had traveled a murky path, one which threatened democracy itself. Lippmann soon drew back from some of his own implications.

Among behavioral psychologists, meanwhile, Harvard professor B. F. Skinner, *Walden Two* (1948) and *Science and Human Behavior* (1953), attracted considerable attention by carrying to logical conclusion current assumptions about human behavior. Walden Two was an imaginary utopia composed of happy men and women guided by a benevolent social engineer knowledgeable in behavioral psychology. Sophisticated technology and an understanding of human behavior were sufficient, Skinner believed, to manipulate people toward socially desirable goals. "The techniques for controlling human behavior were obvious enough," one of Skinner's fictional characters observed. But there was a problem. "The trouble was, they [techniques] were in the hands of the wrong people — or of feeble repair men." This idea was probed more deeply in *Science and Human Behavior*. "Are we to continue to develop a science of human behavior," asked Skinner, "without regard to the use which will be made of it? If not, to whom is the control which it generates to be delegated? This . . . question . . . is a frightening one," declared Skinner, "for there is good reason to fear those who are most apt to seize control." Indeed there was!

Skinner's studies coincided with publication of two frightening novels by Englishman George Orwell, *Animal Farm* (1946) and *1984* (1949). The grim possibilities of human manipulation and exploitation based upon psychological insights and advanced technology were disturbingly revealed by the Big Brother of Oceania.

By the 1940s and 1950s, however, Americans had more than Orwellian novels to arouse fears and anxieties about the prospects of human manipulation. The emergence of fascist totalitarianism in Italy in the 1920s and in Germany in the 1930s, followed by war and the extermination of six million Jews by Nazi overlords, and the realization that totalitarianism also prevailed in Communist Russia, caused many Americans to reassess the intellectual developments of the early twentieth century. Was Nazi Germany a logical result of relativism and the de-emphasis of universal values? Was totalitarianism of the right or left the likely result where political propagandists exploited irrational Freudian impulses or used sophisticated technology to bring about desired conditioned reflexes? Closer to home, popular sociologist Vance Packard, *The Hidden Persuaders* (1957) and *The Waste Makers* (1960), argued that the American public already was being manipulated by Madison Avenue advertisers who, in league with large corporations, fund-raisers, and politicians, cleverly appealed to subliminal drives to sell merchandise, raise money, and elect governors, senators, and presidents.

Many Americans of the post-World War II years, sensing that intellectual changes of the late nineteenth and early twentieth centuries had contributed to the international disorders, clearly desired a more orderly and certain world, one in harmony with universal values. Opposition to relativism was particularly evident in a postwar return to religion. A 1948 opinion poll revealed that 95 percent of those questioned believed in God; 90 percent prayed; 60 percent expected to go to heaven; and 60 percent belonged to a church or synagogue. These were impressive figures, considering that only about 20 percent of the populace had claimed church membership in Abe Lincoln's America. The popular appeal of religion was further indicated by the large crowds attracted by evangelist Billy Graham and the commercial success of the inspirational literature of Norman Vincent Peale, whose *The Power of Positive Thinking* (1952) made best-seller lists. Moreover, in 1952 "God's Float" led the parade at President Eisenhower's first inaugural. Not to be outdone, Congress established a special prayer room in the Capitol, inserted the phrase "under God" into the pledge of allegiance, and had "In God We Trust" inscribed on all coins. And the buxom screen star, Jane Russell, announced: "I love God. And when you get to know Him, you find He's a Livin' Doll."

These popular, but often superficial, expressions of religiosity were paralleled by a more substantive search for absolutes. President Nathan Pusey of Harvard transformed the Harvard Divinity School into a leading theological center by assembling a distinguished faculty which included Reinhold Niebuhr, sometimes dubbed the "Protestant Pope." In his early years Niebuhr had readily embraced the social gospel of Walter Rauschenbusch and the pragmatism of John Dewey. By the early 1940s, having experienced two world wars and a great depression, he had rejected both as being unrealistically optimistic. As a major spokesman for neo-orthodoxy, he stressed absolute values and the tenacity of sin. Although allowing for some human improvement, theologian Niebuhr insisted that sin was universal and inevitable. In Catholic circles Thomas Merton, Bishop Fulton J. Sheen, and Jacques Maritain, a French scholar, were well-received, while Jewish scholar Will Herberg, *Protestant, Catholic and Jew* (1955), won approval by suggesting there was a common ground in all three religions within American culture.

To some extent, the postwar interest in religion, as well as the desire for absolutes, accounted for the favorable reaction to the massive twelve volume study by British historian Arnold Toynbee, *A Study of History* (1933-1961). In attempting to document universal principles underlying the growth and decline of civilizations, Toynbee emphasized the importance of spiritual values. Religion gave cohesion to a civilization, and thereby contributed to its durability. Disintegration of those values hastened decline. Invoking the authority of Toynbee, many clergymen subsequently forecast dire consequences for American civilization unless Americans returned to the spiritual values of their forefathers.

There were also secular manifestations of the desire for a more predictable world resting on absolutes. Some anthropologists, while still viewing cultural relativity as a major accomplishment within their discipline, expressed misgivings after World War II. In 1952 David Bidney, a noted theoretical anthropologist, told an International Symposium on Anthropology that cultural relativists had been so concerned about cultural differences that they failed "to appreciate the polar requirement of a common core of objective values. There can be no mutual respect for differences where there is no community of values also." This remark was partially prompted by the apparent inability of some of Bidney's colleagues, given the concept of cultural relativity, to condemn Nazi Germany or totalitarian Russia.

Another assault on relativism was waged by the New Conservatives of the 1940s and 1950s. While significant differences separated some of the New Conservatives, they all saw a continuous conservative tradition in America from John Adams forward and they all stressed the importance of absolute values. Echoing theologian Niebuhr, Peter Viereck, *Conservatism Revisited* (1949), defined conservatism as "the political secularization of the doctrine of original sin." Political institutions, along with the churches, thought he, restrained the natural man and suited him for society. The New Conservative, Viereck explained, was a creative traditionalist who sought change in ways harmonious with the human need for security and tradition. The Michigan-born educator and writer, Russell Kirk, *The Conservative Mind* (1953), similarly assailed pragmatic relativism, emphasized order and stability, and sanctioned gradual change within the framework of past traditions.

While not identifying with the New Conservatives, Walter Lippmann, *The Public Philosophy* (1955), expressed similar concerns, demonstrating the extent to which his views had shifted since 1913. No longer optimistic about the ability of statesmen to guide the masses and convinced that extreme individualism caused social fragmentation, Lippmann now sought order and continuity through identification of western values with transcendent natural laws. Lippmann further asserted the need for a consensus among the members of society, at least on controversial issues.

This suggestion struck a responsive chord, for already a school of young scholars was busy on a more conservative interpretation of American history. The consensus historians, as these scholars were called, disputed previous interpretations of American history, such as that of Charles Beard, which had highlighted social and economic conflicts. Instead, these writers played down friction and emphasized continuity and consensus. Richard Hofstadter, *The American Political Tradition* (1948), a widely read historian of the 1950s and 1960s, suggested that angry political debate had always been just so much rhetoric, inasmuch as Americans had always been in basic agreement on property rights, economic individualism, and the virtues of competition. In an analysis of American political thought, Louis Hartz, *The Liberal Tradition in America* (1955), concurred in Hofstadter's conclusions. Americans had escaped the extreme fluctuations characteristic of European history, Hartz said, because Americans had always been middle-class, property-conscious individualists. But it was University of Chicago historian Daniel Boorstin, *The Genius of American Politics* (1953), who was perhaps most ebullient about the American consensus. Quite satisfied with the America of the 1950s, Boorstin hailed it "a decent, free, and God-fearing society."

But something was wrong. Religion and New Conservatism, to be sure, had enabled many Americans to recover something of the certainty of the nineteenth century. It was fashionable again to discuss absolute values. Nevertheless, some observers of the 1950s despaired over the emergence of a "mass society." Just as the American past had been "homogenized" by the consensus historians, so also had the present, especially in the suburbs. As a result of the continued rural-to-urban migration, the percentage of urbanites had risen to 64 percent by 1950. Twenty years later the percentage was almost 75 percent, with California now being the most urbanized state in the Union with approximately 91 percent of its populace residing in urban centers. New Jersey (88.9 percent), Rhode Island (87.1 percent), New York (85.5 percent), and Massachusetts (84.6 percent) followed closely behind. Even the traditionally rural South experienced significant urban growth, increasing from 28 percent in 1920 to almost 65 percent in 1970. Although the total population was becoming more urbanized, as these figures reflect, the population of several central cities had actually declined by 1950, signifying a move from the city proper to the surrounding suburbs. The 1970 census revealed that more Americans, for the first time, lived in suburbia. The trend in that direction, noticeable by 1920, had accelerated after World War II. By the 1950s numerous observers, disturbed by the suburban movement, expressed alarm over the growth of a mass society characterized by estrangement, anxiety, and conformity.

Harvard sociologist David Riesman, *The Lonely Crowd* (1953), figured prominently in shaping the popular view of American mass culture. Riesman detected a basic change in the American character. Whereas nineteenth century Americans presumably had been inner-directed individualists, twentieth century Americans had become other-directed conformists. To be sure, this was a change in degree, for other-directed people had existed in the nineteenth century and some inner-directed people still lived. Nevertheless, the present trend was definitely toward other-direction. Riesman explained this environmentally. The nineteenth century had been a job-oriented era. Emphasis had been upon heavy industrial construction and productivity. The values of inner-directed persons coalesced with the needs of the time. Guided by an internalized set of values, the self-reliant and self-confident inner-directed person labored steadfastly to accomplish specific objectives, undisturbed by the opinions of other people. To use Riesman's metaphor, the inner-directed person remained stable and on course, as though steered by a gyroscope. To Riesman, the seventeenth century Puritans and nineteenth century industrial tycoons were classic examples of inner-direction.

By the mid-twentieth century, however, the task of building steel mills, railroads, and the like had been completed. Americans now lived in an urban, consumer-oriented society, one ideally suited for other-direction. Unlike his nineteenth century predecessor, the other-directed person needed and sought group approval, and thus was acutely concerned about the opinions of peers. Whereas the nineteenth century inner-directed businessman needed only a lawyer, an auditor, and an engineer to manage his affairs, the twentieth century other-directed businessman needed a corp of public relations men, labor counselors, and advertisers to get along. Somewhat like a radar set, the other-directed person gleaned surrounding signals and adjusted behavior accordingly. The "invisible hand" of Adam Smith, quipped Riesman, had given way to the "glad hand." Mass conformity resulted. Similarly, author and editor

William H. Whyte, Jr., *The Organization Man* (1956), argued that Americans had forsaken the traditional Protestant ethic, with its emphasis upon self-reliance, hard work, diligence, and individual competition, for a twentieth century social ethic, which encouraged belongingness and togetherness. This new ethic was particularly evident in suburbia, thought Whyte, where organization types sought above all else to get along with people by conforming to peer group opinions. Whyte saw in this anonymous mass shades of *1984*.

The dissenter of the 1950s who perhaps most influenced the youthful radicals of the 1960s and 1970s, however, was sociologist C. Wright Mills, *The Power Elite* (1956). Born in Texas and educated at the Universities of Texas and Wisconsin, Mills spent his brief academic career at Columbia University. Although not taken too seriously in the 1950s, his criticism of American society was readily accepted and amplified by the New Left of the succeeding decade. Mills argued in *The Power Elite* that the United States in *actual* practice was little more democratic than the mass societies of Nazi Germany or totalitarian Russia. Unlike some of his youthful disciples of the 1960s, however, Mills always conceded that American society had not yet descended as far as either of those European mass societies. But the traits of a mass society — passivity by the citizenry, lack of individual opinions, and an inability to resist manipulation by authorities — were increasingly evident in the United States. While the citizenry theoretically controlled the machinery of government, observed Mills, this was not the case in actuality. Americans enjoyed only the form, the illusion, of democracy. Actual power was wielded by a small power elite consisting of corporate, military, and political leaders. And since the public had little information beyond that supplied by the mass media, people, instead of exercising independent and intelligent judgment, thought in terms of stereotypes created by opinion makers. So rather than exercising the theoretical democratic right to govern themselves, the masses were actually manipulated to accept policies desired by the elite. The whole process was especially pernicious, thought Mills, because Americans, given the form of democracy, actually thought they were free.

In *The Causes of World War III* (1958), Mills outlined another theme popular with the anti-Vietnam war critics of the

1960s and 1970s. He attempted to tie the power elite to specific policy decisions regarding armaments. Accepting the premise that World War II had solved the Great Depression, Mills maintained that continued prosperity in the 1950s was due primarily to defense spending. Corporate leaders, especially in the missile, air craft, and electronic industries, supported larger military expenditures, lest the economy suffer recession. Military defense and corporate profits coalesced. The military elite, concerned about its own power and prestige, readily justified more sophisticated weaponry systems. And the political elite easily maneuvered appropriation bills through Congress, claiming that national defense hung in the balance. The tragedy, said Mills, was that this preparation for defense probably would lead to the very war it was supposed to prevent.

After a brief stay in Cuba, Mills wrote *Listen, Yankee* (1960), and again foreshadowed the sentiment of those young radicals who came later in the decade. In this sympathetic account of Fidel Castro's revolution, Mills viewed recent Cuban events pragmatically and relativistically. Batista, the former Cuban leader, had been an oppressive tyrant; Castro, while exercising dictatorial power, was using it in behalf of downtrodden peasants and workers. Land redistribution, educational reform, and other socioeconomic alterations would improve the quality of life for all Cubans. The desirability of these goals enabled Mills to justify the violence, the mass executions, which accompanied Castro's seizure of power. Reflecting a relativistic outlook, Mills asserted that "the purposes and results of killing are quite different in different places and at different times." And lest Americans become overly self-righteous about the killing in Cuba, Mills recalled that Americans, too, had killed as they advanced westward across the continent and beyond.

From 1900 to 1962, when Mills died, American society had undergone significant change. The nation was decidedly more industrial, more urban, more organized, and more suburban. But did these changes in the configuration of society produce the conformity, passivity, anxiety, and estrangement perceived by scholars such as Riesman, Whyte, and Mills? Probably not. This does not mean that contemporary society is free of those conditions. Rather, it suggests that conformity and passivity have deeper roots in American history than recognized by many contemporary social critics. Riesman's assertion, for instance, that nineteenth century Americans were inner-directed was overdrawn. Conformity — the "glad hand" — was as evident to discerning observers of nineteenth century America as it is today. The French analyst of Jacksonian America, Alexis de Tocqueville, described in detail the conformity of the "majority dominated" American. And since there is little difference between de Tocqueville's nineteenth century majority domi- nated person and Riesman's twentieth century other-directed person, American character, it would seem, has not undergone drastic change in the last century and a half. As for Whyte, his charges about suburbia were exaggerated. Recent scholarship proves there is more diversity, less conformity, in the suburbs than Whyte realized. And there is nothing particularly novel about the elements of mass culture, which so disturbed Mills. To be sure, psychological insights into human behavior and sophisticated technology have enhanced the possibilities for manipulation. But in American politics, manipulation as such is at least as old as Alexander Hamilton, Thomas Jefferson, and Aaron Burr. Frontier revivalists, moreover, have always skill- fully moved "sinners" along the "right" path. As for passivity, recent scholars have suggested that voters were as lethargic in the 1780s, when the Constitution was being ratified, as they are today. So despite the drastic material changes which have accompanied the shift from rural-agricultural to urban-industrial America, it is difficult to prove that American society is characterized by more conformity or passivity now than in the last century.

Organization and group action, however, are more evident today than a century ago. From political pressure groups to Ralph Nader's efforts in behalf of sports fans, Americans join associations to achieve a multiplicity of political, economic, charitable, and social objectives. Many clubs and organizations have been necessitated by industrialization and the growth of corporations; they have all been facilitated by urbanization. That Americans are "joiners" is beyond dispute. But it is highly debatable that such group activity makes the twentieth century American any more homogenized than his less-organized nine- teenth century ancestor.

While his arguments were overstated, Mills is still an important figure in the history of ideas. Reminiscent of those reformers and scholars of the early 1900s, he not only defended and encouraged change, but also voiced an intellectual viewpoint long out of style. To some extent, present circumstances determine the acceptance or rejection of ideas. Two world wars, a great depression, the mass extermination of human beings, and apprehension about the future, had caused many post-World War II thinkers to discard ideas popular in the early 1900s, specifically pragmatism and relativism. Among plain people as well as many intellectuals of the 1940s and 1950s, there was a desire for a more orderly and certain world. Emphasis, therefore, was upon absolute, as opposed to relative, values. Mills, meanwhile, disturbed by various trends of the 1950s, gave renewed expression to pragmatism and relativism. In this sense, Mills was a link between the reformers of the early 1900s and the youthful radicals of the 1960s and early 1970s. Intellectual history had moved in something of a circle.

This does not mean that the intellectual climate of the late 1960s and early 1970s was identical to that of 1900. Far from it. Intellectual certainty buttressed by scientific and social theories, as was the case in the late nineteenth century, is irretrievably past. To be sure, the religious revival and the New Conservatism of the 1950s reassured many Americans. Still, clergymen today do not speak with the same intellectual authority as their counterparts of the nineteenth century. And the recent interest in situation ethics reflects a retreat from moral absolutism even among some clergymen. Not only has certainty been eroded somewhat, but, given the probing of Freudian and behavioral psychologists, confidence in human rationality has also been shaken. These same developments and studies, however, have also sharpened our understanding of human behavior. Uncertainty, therefore, need not lead to psychological depression or pessimism, for intellectual developments of the twentieth century have enabled us to understand more clearly human actions, past and present.

SUGGESTED READINGS

The best comprehensive treatments of American social and intellectual history are Ralph Henry Gabriel, *The Course of American Democratic Thought* (1956), Merle Curti, *The Growth of American Thought* (1964), Stow Persons, *American Minds, A History of Ideas* (1958), and Harvey Wish, *Society and*

Thought in Modern America (1962). Other fine studies, especially on social developments, are Carl Degler, *Out of Our Past, The Forces That Shaped Modern America* (1959), and Gilman M. Ostrander, *American Civilization in the First Machine Age, 1890-1940* (1970).

Good accounts of the shifts in American thought at the turn of the twentieth century are Morton White, *Social Thought in America, The Revolt Against Formalism* (1957), Henry F. May, *The End of American Innocence* (1964), Charles Forcey, *The Crossroads of Liberalism* (1967), and Edward C. Moore, *American Pragmatism, Peirce, James, and Dewey* (1961).

Ronald Lora, *Conservative Minds in America* (1971), and Clinton Rossiter, *Conservatism in America* (1962), are able treatments of conservative thought.

Readable accounts of contemporary trends are Ronald Berman, *America in the Sixties, An Intellectual History* (1968), Jeff Nuttall, *Bomb Culture* (1968), and Robert Allen Skotheim, *Totalitarianism and American Social Thought* (1971).

CHAPTER FOUR

The Emergence
of the New South

MARION B. LUCAS

When Jed Tewksbury's mother told him to "leave this place and git as far as you can git" in Robert Penn Warren's *A Place To Come To*, she meant more than just leaving mythical Dugton, Alabama, or the stifling, conservative, atmosphere which permeated his rural and backward county. He was to depart "the South."

Geographically, the South consists of the eleven states of the former Confederacy. Yet, Southern influence and culture has spilled over those borders to taint the "nationalism" of Maryland, West Virginia, Kentucky, and Missouri. But more than geography, the region is an idea; a way of life. It is a concept fixed by soil, climate, the presence of blacks, provincialism, close family relationships, and political domination by a small plutocracy.

The region falls readily into time frames. The first phase is the period from about 1815, when a separate "South" began, through the Civil War. A second phase consists of the years 1865-1932, a period of leadership crisis. The third, the decades from 1932 to 1965, were years of flux in Southern history. The fourth, 1965 to the present, is the period which has seen "the South" acquire a new and favorable image as the "Sun Belt."

The Civil War and Reconstruction had the unfortunate effect of fixing certain ideas in the minds of Southerners; concepts that have not been easily changed. Political Reconstruction was scarcely over before the myth that the South had "won every battle, but the Radicals took it away from us during Reconstruction" was prevalent throughout the region. The Radical Reconstruction constitutions were the most democratic the Southern states have ever had, but the presence of reformers and their elevation of blacks confirmed Southern opposition to everything Northern. Indeed, to many education, hospitals, social programs, progress, and democracy, because they were associated with the North and Reconstruction, were damn Yankee tricks and therefore wrong.

This suspicion of outside ideas created a defensiveness, a feeling of persecution, and a sense of inferiority in many Southern minds that would make the words "the South" conjure up an unfavorable image in the minds of most Northerners. For 100 years visiting Northerners, in typical provincial fashion, would see everything back home as better. They would find the language peculiar, the institutions ante-diluvian, and more poverty than they were willing to admit existed at home, but would remember the people as friendly.

A major problem for Southerners in the years after the war was that their old leaders were proscribed from government. Seeing carpetbaggers, scalawaggers, and blacks eliminated from politics, and their old planter leaders — the Hamptons, Barbours, and Byrds — back in power became a goal for red dirt farmers and their village allies. But the return of their old leaders to power would have a deeper meaning in that it would symbolize the resumption of white supremacy.

When, by early 1877, control had been wrested from the last of the Radical administrations, into the positions of authority marched the South's leadership of the future — the merchant-planters. They were a combination of old planters, who contributed their names, and rising businessmen who were as Republican in economic principles as Thad Stevens and Mark Hanna. Under their leadership white supremacy came to mean merchant-planter supremacy, not the supremacy of the poor farmer, the artisan, and the mill worker. These groups would be held in line by the race issue which became the "red herring" of Southern politics for 100 years. Ironically, blacks, who were shortly prohibited from voting, would be "the issue" in deciding most Southern elections.

The "Bourbon" leaders of the New South, an epithet hurled

at them because they, like the restored French kings, seemed to have "learned nothing and forgotten nothing," looked north-eastward for guidance following the Civil War. They possessed an economic philosophy which promoted capitalism, and represented in their administrations only merchant-planters, local industrialists, and rising businessmen. They wanted high tariffs and hand-outs from government; they fought against organized labor and the regulation of business. They rode into office on the votes of the common white people to whom they appealed through race prejudice, through corruption of the ballot box, and, curiously, through the use of black votes. Once in power they preached retrenchment. Cheap local and state government became a fetish. Alexander Hamilton's philosophy had won the South, and in doing so, Southern leaders turned their backs on the people. Their leadership benefited only themselves. They advocated social Darwinism in business and life; money became the new measure of wealth, while morals suffered, education languished, and social programs were anathema.

A great opportunity was missed during the first twenty-five years following the Civil War. The region had an opportunity to start over, to learn from the experiences of the North, to almost literally build from the ground up. In a free country which possessed a free press with only self-imposed regulation, the South should have been able to adopt some of the more humanizing aspects of Northern society. But the leadership that emerged appeared incapable of seeing the evils that existed in Southern society.

By the 1890s a great common-man discontent had developed known as the Populist movement. People had grown to hate their Bourbon "redeemers" for two reasons. The Bourbons were the friends of the hated trusts, and they had inherited from the Radicals control over blacks. On more than one occasion Bourbons had purchased enough black votes to have their way. But there were other legitimate complaints: declining commodity prices, decreasing land values, fore-closures, a shortage of banks, and inadequate capital.

"Grass roots" demagogues began preaching hatred of "the money power," "the trusts," and "the hirelings of Wall Street" and virtually calling for a class war. There was some talk among Populist leaders of common cause with blacks, but fear of their elevation to competition with whites outweighed the oppression of class. Consequently, most "populists," fearing a third party that might give black Republicans the balance of power, struggled for control of the Democratic party. Bourbons and Populists fought it out in the "white" Democratic primary with the winner assured of victory in the general election.

As erroneously as the Physiocrats before them and the Vanderbilt Agrarians who were to follow, the Populists clung to the idea that only farmers produce, that other people are parasites who live off the agrarian worker. Rather than facing the real problems of the one-crop system, the tenant system, unbridled business, and generally poor government, Populists looked for scapegoats. And when they failed to come up with answers, common-man leaders such as "Pitchfork" Ben Tillman quickly learned to soothe their constituents with racist dogma while they silently adopted the policies of the Bourbon leaders they supplanted. They kept their names in the headlines with their criticism of the North and quietly sold out to the moneyed interests behind the scene.

From the 1890s to the 1930s, about the only things that grew readily, and into bountiful crops in the South, were demagogues. Worse than weeds, they sprung up everywhere in ever-increasing numbers.

What the demagogue needs, though Joseph McCarthy showed it is not absolutely· required, is an ignorant and uneducated electorate. Here the region excelled. "What you really need," the demagogue's speech went, "was not book-learnin', but common sense." Coleman L. "Coley" Blease of South Carolina expressed his opposition to public education in this way: "I have never heard a common sense argument in favor of it." The implication was clear.

Public education was the single biggest failure of the South, and remains today one of its largest problems. The truth is that the region did not believe in public education. Only a handful of Southern states actually established a system of public schools before the Civil War, and then mostly on paper. The schools established by the Reconstruction governments were promptly allowed to die, and what remained was a woefully financed system which was public in name only. The blacks were especially neglected. South Carolina, for instance, had only one high school for blacks in 1918.

In response to criticism from without, Southern states often pointed to their rapidly increasing expenditure for public schools, but their programs always looked better on paper than they actually were. Statistics do lie when the number of pupils and teachers, say in 1879, are given, and it is not pointed out that the school year was less than 100 days. The only thing that kept Southern schools going in the post-Civil War period was Northern philanthropy such as the George Peabody Fund, the Slater fund, and the General Education Board of John D. Rockefeller.

The results of the lack of an adequate educational system was economic backwardness that begs description. The wage-labor gang system of farming established just after the war, with blacks working under an overseer, was entirely too unimaginative and doomed to early failure. Its replacement, the share crop and share tenant system, with its accompanying lien laws which gave the landlord first claim to the crop, was the old plantation system under a new name. It was as exploitative and wasteful of human resources as slavery had been, but with one difference. Under these systems both whites and blacks were reduced to economic bondage and, in some states, were virtually serfs. The result was a steady decline in initiative and an increase in shiftlessness among farmers.

The presence of impoverished farmers, both black and white, offered prospective factory owners a ready source of laborers once industrialization began. Two compelling reasons led Northern factory owners to build in the South or to buy out foundering factories established by local citizens with inadequate capital. Southern labor was both cheap and docile. And further, New South leaders made numerous concessions to businessmen and industrialists. Public officials who allowed convict labor to be worked at a cost of seven cents a day in privately owned coal mines created an attitude that was conducive to profits. Consequently, Southern wages remained low, running thirty to forty percent behind those in the North through the first three decades of the twentieth century.

During the early years of the twentieth century, a new group of leaders emerged in the South known as the Progressives. They were moderate Democrats who blended more readily into the National Democratic party of the Woodrow Wilson era. They were, for the most part, educated men of solid middle class roots. Nevertheless, they were idolized by the rank and file. These politicians, closer to the cities than to the countryside in background, took advantage of the illiteracy, provincialism, weak social institutions, the one-party system, exploitation by Northern capitalists, and the race issue to build powerful, self-perpetuating political machines.

The twentieth century demagogues were a bizarre group of individuals. James K. Vardaman, the "White Chief," who dressed in pure white and whose long black hair flowed to his shoulders, campaigned from a white lumber wagon, drawn by white oxen. Theodore G. "The Man" Bilbo, a former theological student and school teacher, once admitted accepting a bribe of $645, and was said to have "a cunning common to criminals which passed for intelligence." Coley Blease, who always dressed in a frock coat, striped trousers, and a shoe-string tie, gave the state of South Carolina the worst government it has ever had; yet, he was beloved by the people.

These and other demagogues deliberately cultivated outlandish manners, used violent language and stunts to attract attention, boasted of their prejudices and their humble background, and deliberately appealed to the pride and bigotry of their "lint head" and "redneck" constituency.

While the names of Southern Progressives can be associated with a number of reform measures in the United States Congress, when it came to the race issue their slogan was "No Negroes Allowed." To be sure, racism, disenfranchisement, and segregation had existed to some degree since 1865, but there was a much more lenient attitude in the years before 1890. With the rise of the demagogues — first the Populists and then the Progressives — what had formerly been left to custom became laws aimed at making their fellow Southerners, the blacks, second class citizens. In an outburst of state legislation, city ordinances, and other local "rules and regulations" that often took on the force of law, segregation and disenfranchisement laws were passed throughout the South after 1890, making the period the black man's nadir. Within a few short years signs of "white only" appeared everywhere. A 1914 code in one state prohibited whites and blacks from working in the same room and using the same entrances, pay windows, exits, doorways, stairs, lavatories, toilets, drinking buckets, pails, cups, and glasses. These laws remained in force until the 1960s.

The effect of the failure of leadership was to make the South, during the depths of the depression, the poorest region of the nation. It remained provincial, sensitive to outside criticism, and to Yankee ideas. And as at other times, when a call for reform was heard, it was conservative rather than liberal, looking to the past rather than the future.

In 1930 a small group of writers centered in the English Department at Vanderbilt University published *I'll Take My Stand*, an agrarian manifesto which denounced the multi-evils of industrialization and the problems that stemmed from urbanization. The South, Donald Davidson, John Crowe Ransom and Robert Penn Warren maintained, should do what it does best — farm. It was the agrarian way of life that gave the South its distinct characteristics, that made the South rural, stable, conservative, and religious. They defended race prejudice and denounced "modernism" in religion and the emerging importance of sociology. Southern institutions, they maintained, should remain as they were.

It was not that the Vanderbilt Agrarians had no good ideas. Indeed, their suspicions of the effect of industrialization on both society and its environment were points well taken. It is indeed a shame that Southern leadership did not pick up on these points, at least at a later date. But the problem of the South in 1932 was that it suffered from the very point the Agrarians were fostering — too much farming.

What the South needed was a new approach that looked to the future. The region's strengths were many. The National Emergency Council on the Economic Conditions of the South in 1938 showed great natural resources: many soils, favorable climate, plentiful rain, extensive forests, abundant wildlife, numerous rivers, adequate power, and improving roads. And even more, there were better than adequate human resources. Nevertheless, the region was the poorest in the country.

What was wrong with the Southern region of the United States? The National Emergency Council concluded that there were essentially three major causes of this condition. One was agricultural and stemmed from farm tenancy and the one-crop system. A second was industrial and resulted from the cruder nature of Southern industry, unfair freight rates, and absentee ownership. And finally, there was the financial cause. The region suffered from a shortage of banks, and being poorer, had less to offer as collateral, with the result being higher interest rates. The consequences of these conditions were poor health conditions, inadequate housing (the NEC estimated 50 percent of Southerners should be re-housed), low educational standards, and the emigration of economically productive people out of the South.

Fortunately for the South, a new approach came along in the 1930s. What the South needed, Rupert Vance and Howard Odum of the Regional School of the University of North Carolina at Chapel Hill maintained, was to emphasize agriculture where the land was best suited for that purpose, while simultaneously developing those areas best suited for industry. Essentially, what Regionalists were saying was that the South would be better off with a diversity of interests in agriculture and a balanced economy. They argued that farming of marginal lands should be eliminated.

To give up agriculture where it was unprofitable, they held, would not destroy "sectional" culture which should be preserved, but within a national compass. The New Deal administration of Franklin D. Roosevelt turned to the Regionalists who were most influential in governmental planning for the South. Their ideas dominated the thinking of what the region should be through the 1970s.

While hard economic struggles occupied center stage during the period, the South was also going through a "constitutional revolution" in civil rights. After suffering a setback in the 1935 *Grovey* v. *Townsend* decision which allowed continued exclusion of blacks from white-controlled Democratic primaries, a new avenue of attack opened for blacks in 1941. In *U.S.* v. *Classic* the Supreme Court held that the federal government could regulate state primary elections. This led blacks in Texas to begin a suit that culminated in the monumental *Smith* v. *Allwright* case in 1944 which finally opened primaries to blacks. An attempt to subvert the decision ended in failure in the 1947 *Elmore* v. *Rice* decision. A simultaneous attack on segregation culminated in the destruction of the "separate but equal" concept in 1954 in *Brown* v. *Board of Education of Topeka*.

Time for the South to work out its racial problems was rapidly running out. The old comment, "if outside agitators would leave us alone, we would get along all right down here," would no longer suffice. Time had already been too long, and all but the most myopic should have seen the handwriting on the wall. Politicians who shouted "segregation now and forever" were speaking to an ever-diminishing crowd.

Three conditions existed that would make change inevitable. One was increasing pressure against the segregation system by blacks, led by ministers and college students. Their methods were passive resistance. It was slow and there were numerous setbacks, but when the thirty years of agitation is placed beside the three hundred years of past wrong-doings, it was remarkably fast.

A second condition was the emergence of an increasingly educated white population, many of whom were liberals. Behind the scenes these reasonable people worked to end the embarrassment of racial injustice. Whites who grew up in the Southern cities knew how complete segregation and disenfranchisement of blacks really was. In much of the deep South every third person a white met on the street was black; yet the gulf between the races was such that their paths never really crossed. In the rural areas of the South liberal whites saw the constant humiliation of blacks by local employers and officials as discomforting.

Eventually, critics in the tradition of W. J. Cash and Clarence Cason would not only say their piece, but also would remain to hear the rebuttal. Southern writers dominated the literature of the twentieth century and more and more their works were filled with none-too-subtle criticisms of Southern society. There is, for instance, a steady sympathy for the suffering of the black people in the writings of William Faulkner. Something had to be done, and when it was, both blacks and whites realized they were better off.

But there was a third condition which led to change in Southern attitudes on race — outside pressure from the North, without which there would have been few meaningful changes in the South. Southern reform leaders have never been able to find a following sufficient to win elections. For a majority of Southerners the Fair Employment Practices Commission would never be anything but an evil idea "hatched in the brains of Communists," and the Civil Rights bills would always remain the "demands of parlor pinks and subversives." For these people "Washington" became the scapegoat. All reversals, economic, racial, or personal, could be blamed on the "briefcase toting egg-heads" of Washington. Anyone who suggested change in the South was an outside agitator. The pressure was steady, however, and it was a Southwesterner, Lyndon B. Johnson, who was finally responsible for the two major measures that completely changed the region — the Civil Rights Act of 1964 and the Voting Rights Act of 1965.

The years since 1965 have been years of astounding change for the South. There is no question but that the region has joined, to a great extent, the mainstream of America. The old image of backwardness and racial oppression has faded with increasing speed as one approaches the present; and in its place the South has taken its seat in the "Sun Belt," a political and economic grouping which stretches from North Carolina to San Francisco, roughly along the thirty-seventh parallel southward to the border.

Why the term "Sun Belt" is so readily, and favorably, acceptable is difficult to assess. Perhaps it has grown out of the desire of many Northerners who prefer to live in the comfortable climate of the region to think of their new home in favorable terms. Others, no doubt, see the "Sun Belt" as a new frontier where there is a slower pace of life when compared with crowded, decaying Northern cities and energy shortages.

The great economic development which began in the South during World War II has continued. But the steady flow of Northern capital southward has been accompanied by several major changes. For the first time Northerners are moving with their industries with the result that more of the profits are remaining in the South. Further, the quality of the industries being developed in the South has improved, and some states, finally learning from the mistakes of Northern industrial areas, are attempting to choose more desirable industries. Highly skilled industries such as aerospace, electronics, and defense are taking their place in the South beside agri-business.

With more emphasis on business, and the decline of segregation in the South, there has been a concomitant growth of the Republican party in the region. As the Democratic party inched steadily toward the left in the 1960s, the conservative and the right wing, "redneck" element within the party, became increasingly uncomfortable. Having always been Republican in everything but name, they found it easy during the 1960s and 1970s to join the Republican party. With the sincere conservatives went the lunatic fringe embarrassments like Strom Thurmond who switched to the Republican party in 1964. The unfortunate result has been that the Republican party in the South has become, on occasion, comparable in policy and leadership to the demagogues of the turn of the century in that it often does not offer a viable alternative.

The abandonment of the Democratic party by many of the conservatives allowed moderate and liberal white Democrats to join with blacks to form a new coalition which has tended to be the majority in Southern states at election time. This new Democratic coalition, only slightly less liberal than its Northern counterpart, has for the first time placed the South squarely within the ideology of the Democratic party. And with the emergence of "liberal" Jimmy Carter, it appears Southern Democrats will have a strong position in the national Democratic party for years.

Though Southern society has moved closer to that of the North in the 1970s, the region remains, in many ways, a continuing paradox. Family ties are strong, yet the population has become increasingly cosmopolitan and mobile. And while conservatism in theology is dominant, the Bible Belt is at last awakening to the social gospel. With regard to the races, the end of segregation in public places seems to have led to an attitude of accommodation between blacks and whites, though a gulf still separates them socially.

Nor has the South lost many of the characteristics that make its place unique in American history. Its slower way of life, its embedded conservatism, and its sense of the past, though in a struggle that threatens to end many regional differences, continue to survive. Nevertheless, the future of the South is brighter today than at anytime since the Civil War. With recent developments in improving public education, an embryonic two-party system, the growth of a diversified economy, the end of racial segregation and the acceptance of the mainstream of American thought, the South of the "Sun Belt" offers new hope for all its citizens.

SUGGESTED READINGS

Kenneth M. Stampp's work, *The Era of Reconstruction, 1865-1877* (1965) is a good starting point on the immediate post-Civil War period. C. Vann Woodward's *Origins of the New South* (1951) is the most complete survey of the years 1877-1913 by one of the region's finest scholars. *The Emergence of the New South, 1913-1945* (1967) by George B. Tindall is the best general work on that period, and Theodore Saloutos has exhibited excellent insight in *Farmer Movements in the South 1865-1933*. Charles P. Roland's *The Improbable Era: The South Since World War II* (1975) is the best survey of the period after 1945.

AMERICAN POLITICS AND FOREIGN POLICY

ONE OF THE MAJOR TRENDS in twentieth century America has been the accelerated pace in the growth of the federal government. The first national budget of George Washington's administration (1789-1791) called for the expenditure of $4.3 million. It was not until 1892 that Congress authorized the spending of more than one billion dollars in a single session. By 1977, the annual federal budget has exceeded $400 billion per year. Over $100 billion of that revenue was spent on national defense. Even considering the impact of inflation in this century, the growth of the federal government in terms of expenditure and size has been nothing short of phenomenal. The two factors that most account for the rise of the national government's role in American society in this century have been the increased role of government in counter-balancing the power of big business and the greater American involvement in world diplomacy and international conflicts. The essays in this section indicate the changing and increased position of the federal government in responding to the domestic and foreign challenges which America has faced in the past seventy-five years.

J. Michael Shahan focuses on the reform orientation of the Progressive Era and the New Deal to explain the dynamics which contributed to the growth of government in the twentieth century. While he rejects the traditional definition of reform as good overcoming evil, Shahan maintains that reform has ordered and bureaucratized American society and set the stage for the creation of a modern welfare state. In his analysis, Shahan offers a thoughtful and challenging examination of the importance of reform in American life. In the second essay, Frank Abbott traces the increased involvement of the United States in international affairs. Concentrating on the American entrance into World Wars I and II, Abbott contends that the nation's reaction to the European crises of 1914-1918 and 1939-1945 was determined as much by domestic events as by external forces. He maintains that the rural-urban division in American society played an important part in the United States response to the wars. The third essay by William MacDonald examines the origin and development of the Cold War from 1945 to the present. After reviewing the current debate on who was primarily responsible for the onset of the Cold War, MacDonald concentrates on the forces that have led to a lessening of tension between the United States and the Soviet Union. He analyzes the orientation and strategy of Henry Kissinger in an effort to explain why detente has largely replaced conflict in Soviet-American relations in the past decade. The final essay by David Lee appropriately attempts to trace the impact of reform and foreign policy on the federal government. The main thrust of the essay is to document the growth of presidential power in relation to the legislative and judicial branches of government. Lee contends that the impact of the federal government's increased involvement in the areas of domestic reform and international affairs has caused the expansion of the executive power to such an extent that the president now threatens the very basis of constitutional government. Lee maintains, however, that the excesses of the Watergate scandal have now mobilized forces within the government and the society which are in the process of checking the inordinate powers which the executive has assumed since the 1930s. The four essays outline the dramatic changes in domestic and foreign affairs which the American people and its national government have experienced in the last seventy-five years.

President Theodore Roosevelt speaking at Evanston, Illinois, 1904. (Library of Congress)

CHAPTER FIVE

Political Reform from Roosevelt to Roosevelt

J. MICHAEL SHAHAN

The subject of reform has to a large extent determined the substance and character of twentieth century American politics. From Theodore Roosevelt's modest "Square Deal" proposals through Lyndon Johnson's ambitious vision of the "Great Society," political debate in the United States has often focused upon the need for change and argued the merits of various programs designed to improve, in the view of their proponents, some aspect of American life. The advocates of change have had more success than their opponents and, as a consequence, the role and function of government in the United States has changed drastically from what it was in 1900. Americans have replaced the idea that governmental power should extend no further than the protection of life and property with the concept of the modern bureaucratic state in which government has the responsibility for harmonizing and ordering the entire industrial economy. As a result, governmental power has increased and the average citizen now comes into daily contact with a government that provides such diverse services as medicare and farm price supports.

The expansion of this bureaucratic state has been tremendous since World War II, but the struggle to win full acceptance of the concept took place during the four decades preceding the attack on Pearl Harbor. From the presidency of Theodore

Roosevelt through that of his distant cousin Franklin Roosevelt, politicians and the public grappled with a variety of problems that originated with America's transition from a rural, agrarian nation to a modern industrial power. The role of government in coping with new problems such as the growth of trusts and the exploitation of child labor was the most prevalent focus of discussion, but there was more at stake than the mere extension of local, state, and federal authority. America was transforming herself into an urban-industrial state and that transformation brought changes not only in governmental power, but also in economic and social organization. The reform movements that were so important in the early decades of the twentieth century cannot be properly understood nor can their impact be gauged without viewing them as an integral part of the process of modernization.

The first historians who attempted to understand this era accepted the reform movements as an important feature of American development, but they tended to view them as separate entities and to divide reform into two waves: the Progressive Era and the New Deal. The progressive movement encompassed the years from 1900 to 1918, and according to the older interpretation it involved a struggle between the forces of good and evil. Taking the rhetoric of the reformers at face value, historians explained progressivism as a contest that pitted the interests of the people — ordinary, hardworking citizens — against the corrupt and rapacious influence of big business, personified by the all-powerful trusts. From this perspective it was easy to interpret the legislative enactments of the prewar period as victories of the people. The accomplishments appeared to be impressive. Besides restricting the power of the trusts and regulating the food and drug industries, the people — acting through the government — extended control over railroads, began a program to conserve natural resources, reformed the banking system, imposed a graduated income tax, and won the right to select United States senators by direct election.

For those who accept this interpretation, World War I marked both the ultimate success of progressivism and its demise. In their rush to win the war and make the world safe for democracy, Americans placed the public interest above private concerns and thus accomplished the ultimate goal of progressivism — the triumph of the people. This victory, however, also spelled defeat for the movement. Progressives were disillusioned by the peace that followed the war, they were repelled by the hatred and bigotry which war unleashed, and they saw in the prosperity and crass materialism of the twenties the restoration of big business to its throne of power and influence.

The crash of 1929 and the ensuing depression, however, brought an abrupt end to the reign of business and set the stage for the second wave of reform, Franklin Roosevelt's New Deal. Assuming command at the darkest hour of economic crisis, Roosevelt developed and secured the enactment of a series of domestic reforms which brought about drastic changes in American life. Big business was dethroned and regulated, the labor movement was recognized and strengthened, and the federal government undertook a multitude of programs for the benefit of the people: social security, public power projects, farm subsidies, federal home loans, federal insurance for bank deposits, and federal relief projects. The concept of the general-welfare state became firmly entrenched and the federal government was committed to actively promoting the public good. It was, in historian Carl Degler's words, a "Third American Revolution."

This view of twentieth century reform, although constructed on a sound factual foundation, is too simplistic in that it fails to critically evaluate the accomplishments of the reformers and does not examine reform in the context of overall development. The progressive era did produce a great deal of legislation, but it is naive to think that this legislation represented nothing more than the will of an aroused public that suddenly demanded social and economic justice for all citizens. Similarly, it is a distortion of reality to idealize the New Deal as the ultimate triumph of public over private concerns. Reform was both more and less than it seemed.

The reform movements of the early twentieth century which collectively came to be known as progressivism involved much more than the sudden awakening of the public conscience. They were part of a complex reaction which Samuel Hays has labeled "the response to industrialism." Examining the period from 1885 to 1914, Hays argued that the social, economic, and political movements of those years composed an

attempt "to cope with industrial change in all its ramifications."
The challenge was immense. The development of industry and
the growth of big business upset the established order and posed
new problems that defied simple solutions. Businessmen occupied unaccustomed positions of status and leadership, but
they had little real control over the system which pushed them
to the top. National and international market factors over
which individuals had little influence determined business
decisions and competitive pressures pushed profits to disas-
trously low levels. Farmers began to realize that they were
contributing a smaller proportion of the national wealth, and
they were bewildered by the commercial marketplace and the
power of giant business concerns. Workers discovered that they
were replaceable and powerless cogs in the production process,
relegated to an urban environment of poverty, inadequate
housing, disease, and despair.

The progressive movement was only one of the reactions to
industrial change, but it proved to be the most significant.
Unlike the workers who joined the utopian Knights of Labor in
the 1880s or the agrarian protesters who rallied under the
banner of Populism in the 1890s, progressives accepted industrialization as a necessary part of progress. Their programs did
not look to the past in the hope of halting or reversing the
economic transformation. Instead, they looked to the future
and sought to reconcile industrialization with the values and
institutions of a capitalist republic. Progressivism was not a
crusade of good against evil or a battle between the people and
special interests. It was a collection of varied, sometimes
contradictory, attempts to meet the challenges posed by
industrialization. Progressive reformers, however, shared one
commitment — a belief that governmental action was necessary
to solve the problems of the day.

Because progressivism was so diverse and embraced so many
different reform programs, it is difficult to pinpoint its source
of support or to generalize about the type of people which the
movement attracted. During the 1950s, George E. Mowry and
Richard Hofstadter made the first serious attempts to profile
the progressive reformers. Using the technique of collective
biography, they each examined the background of prominent
progressive leaders in order to find common characteristics that
might explain the motivation for reform. Their findings reveal

that most of the reformers came from a middle class environment and were well-educated by the standards of the day. The majority were urban-dwelling native Protestants with careers in business or one of the professions. Having identified the "typical" progressive, Mowry and Hofstadter argued that the support for reform originated in status anxieties. Upset because their power and influence was being superseded by business barons like John D. Rockefeller, the middle class progressives embraced reforms that were designed to check the power of big business while preserving the comfortable values of the past. They wanted to regulate business, they supported efforts to eliminate corruption and make politics more democratic, and they felt that meliorative action should be undertaken to improve the lot of the masses.

This interpretation was an important step beyond the simple "people against the interests" argument advanced earlier and it tried to view reform as part of the social adjustment to economic change, but it has serious weaknesses. Studies of those who opposed progressive reforms reveal that the opposition generally shared the same middle class background which supposedly generated the reform impulse. Equally damaging is evidence that indicates that the reformers were not always frustrated in achieving power and status. Many were quite successful and occupied the upper rungs of the social ladder. These findings suggest that the motivation for reform was too complex to be explained in terms of simple dichotomies.

A more sophisticated and persuasive interpretation of the origins of reform has been offered by Robert H. Wiebe who argues that progressivism expressed the needs and desires of a "new middle class." This growing group, rather than being at odds with the economic transformation, consisted of professionals and specialists who thrived in the urban-industrial environment that was taking shape. They rejected the personal, small town value system of the nineteenth century and turned to bureaucratic values that were more in tune with the new era. Economic change was breaking down the barriers of provincial isolation and creating a dynamic, interdependent society. The new middle class accepted this transition and adopted bureaucratic values because they promised order, efficiency, and predictability that the new socio-economic system lacked. The progressive movement embodied the attempt by this new middle class to restructure American life along bureaucratic lines.

Translated into more concrete terms, the involvement of members of the rising professional and business class in the reform movements of the early twentieth century left progressivism with a deep conservative orientation. Many suggestions for change did originate with individuals and groups who perceived themselves as the victims of industrialization and sought some way of improving their position, but the implementation of these suggestions required at least the tacit approval of those who held economic and political power. Although the early calls for antitrust action, labor legislation, and welfare programs often envisioned restructuring society's power relationships, the decision-makers were seldom inclined to surrender their authority and control. However, they were aware of discontent among the lower classes and were frightened by the possibility that "radical" movements such as Populism would increase in size and militancy. Under these circumstances, the more enlightened members of the middle and upper classes, led by the new middle class, saw reform as a means of quieting discontent and radicalism while stabilizing the social order with bureaucratic values. Rather than being a comprehensive program to remake society, progressivism was conservative in that it accepted change as the way to preserve the existing capitalist system.

Although the conservative character of reform was very visible at the local and state level, its most profound impact was upon national policy. The administrations of Theodore Roosevelt, William Howard Taft, and Woodrow Wilson each addressed reform in its own way, but they displayed a uniform commitment to conservative action. In spite of democratic rhetoric and boasts of victories for the people, none of these presidents did anything to endanger the prevailing economic or social order. They did support change, but it was conservative change designed to strengthen the existing system by modifying it to meet the requirements of the emerging urban-industrial society. The necessary adjustments required government to become more active and to assume new responsibilities; however, they did not dictate a redistribution of power or a fundamental change in the economic system.

No individual was more closely identified with the progressive movement at the national level than President Theodore Roosevelt. His call for the Square Deal, his reputation as a trustbuster, and his 1912 campaign for the "New Nationalism" placed him at the head of the progressive ranks and labeled him as one of the leading reformers of the day. Roosevelt did endorse change and pose as the champion of the people, but he was at heart a conservative. Born into a wealthy, established family, Roosevelt was neither a victim of industrialization nor a promoter of the economic transformation. He was a patrician, an upperclass gentleman who defied the social niceties of the late nineteenth century by entering the rough and tumble world of politics. Unable to identify either with the masses or the thriving business and professional class, Roosevelt saw himself as an agent of moderation and social progress. He was opposed to any form of radicalism and was willing to accept change that would strengthen the capitalist system by reducing frustration among the lower classes and checking the abuse of power by those at the upper level of society.

An enthusiastic, aggressive person who relished the exercise of power, Roosevelt captured the public mood and imagination with a vigorous administration that left an impression of achievement. He won acclaim from the public for opposing the trusts, advocating the conservation of natural resources, and supporting social justice legislation such as child labor laws. During his tenure of office, business regulation expanded with the increased use of the Sherman Antitrust Act, the establishment of a Bureau of Corporations, and the passage of the Pure Food and Drug Act, the Meat Inspection Act, and the Hepburn Act. Under the leadership of Chief Forester Gifford Pinchot, the federal government strengthened its commitment to the scientific management and development of the nation's natural wealth and expanded its conservation efforts. Congressional action on social justice measures was minimal, partly because Roosevelt was reluctant to push for pro-labor legislation that he felt bordered on radicalism, but some humanitarian reforms did become law.

Despite the fact that Roosevelt lent rhetorical support to reform and always appeared active, the actual accomplishments of his administration were limited and were well within the boundaries of conservative thought. An astute politician, Roosevelt was aware of public concern over the growth of big business, and he realized that there was strong support for outlawing large business combinations. His well-publicized prosecution of the Northern Securities Company pleased those who wanted antitrust action, and the organization of the Bureau of Corporations seemed to promise strict regulation that would help smaller businesses compete with the giant companies. In reality, the president did little to reverse the trend toward business consolidation. He believed large corporations to be an inevitable result of economic growth and was opposed to their wholesale dissolution. He did use the antitrust act to prosecute cases in which big business had abused its power, but those prosecutions were relatively few in comparison to the number of firms operating.

Government regulation via the Bureau of Corporations was much more to Roosevelt's liking because it gave the government a chance to address the trust question in a positive manner. The Bureau's power to investigate and publicize questionable corporate practices could be used to persuade the corporations to operate on an ethical and fair basis and would allow antitrust action to be reserved as a last resort against corporate recalcitrance. The larger corporations initially opposed the Bureau's interference, but their hostility was short-lived. It soon became apparent that the new agency was not interested in destroying trusts, and the larger business concerns learned to use it to their advantage by relying upon regulation to supply the stability that was needed in the competitive marketplace. Roosevelt was able to pose as the leading antagonist of the trusts while doing little to limit their growth.

President Roosevelt's actions in other areas followed a similar pattern of bold appearances and conservative accomplishments. He threw his support behind the Hepburn Act which gave the Interstate Commerce Commission expanded jurisdiction and the power to set reasonable railroad rates. This bill marked a significant advance in federal regulation of private industry, but it was not as drastic a measure as some wanted. Given the widespread resentment of the railroads and their practices, government ownership was not beyond the realm of possibility. The Hepburn Act provided an alternative to that extreme while satisfying the public demand for action. It also overcame the objections of most railroad leaders by providing for judicial review of all I.C.C. decisions, a safeguard against radical action. The pure food and drug regulation that passed with Roosevelt's endorsement appeased an irate public and improved the quality of some products without causing undue hardships within the industry. Because Roosevelt's conservation policy stressed the efficient, scientific use of natural resources rather than mere preservation, it won the support of large mining and lumbering interests who worked hand in hand with the government to exploit the potential of the nation's public lands. The president's incessant activity and his skillful use of the rhetoric of reform helped defuse popular discontent, but his policies did not threaten the new industrial order.

Despite this conservatism, the Roosevelt administration was responsible for instituting an important change in American life. In order to curb the excesses of business and minimize the appeal of radicalism, the president had to expand the power of the federal government. This expansion did not endanger the sanctity of private property or challenge the social structure of the day, and by later standards the government's new role was not large. It was significant, however, because it gave the federal government, especially the executive branch, new responsibility for supervising business activity and promoting the welfare of its citizens. For better or worse, Theodore Roosevelt laid the foundation for the rise of the bureaucratic welfare state.

The interesting aspect of Roosevelt's accomplishment is that it had the support of a number of businessmen. Although some members of the business community did cling to the nineteenth century concept of laissez-faire and oppose the extension of federal authority, the new middle class led the more farsighted business executives in welcoming government intervention as a means of institutionalizing needed bureaucratic values. Federal regulation was desirable because it would supersede contradictory state laws and provide uniformity for those who operated on a national scale. Government agencies such as the Bureau of Corporations and the Forestry Service could be a valuable adjunct to private business by promoting efficiency and applying expertise to complex problems. Business had to sacrifice the concept of unregulated competition in order to attain the desired stability, but many enlightened businessmen had already concluded that cutthroat competition was counterproductive. Railroads, for example, were willing to accept reasonable rate regulation that would help insure a profit, eliminate the need for costly rate wars and rebates, and make long-term planning easier. The extension of governmental power, rather than a victory of the people over business, was a step toward rationalizing and ordering the new industrial economy.

This process of modernization continued under the leadership of Woodrow Wilson. The southern-born son of a Presbyterian clergyman, Wilson rose to prominence first as a scholar and president of Princeton University and then as governor of New Jersey. A conservative Democrat in his early years, Wilson was never able to make the transition to radical reformer. He did become a key figure in the progressive movement, but like Theodore Roosevelt, his commitment to reform was limited. Although he had little sympathy for the programs of "extremists," he was concerned about the growing power of big business. Wilson was willing to accept change that would help preserve the democratic capitalist system in which he believed.

The presidential campaign of 1912 allowed Wilson to present his ideas to the people and challenge Roosevelt's domination of the reform movement. After securing the Democratic nomination, Wilson ran on the "New Freedom" platform which emphasized the virtues of individualism, competition, and freedom. The program offered little to the advocates of social justice legislation, but it held out hope to those who wanted to reverse the trend toward business consolidation. Because of his strong opposition to monopolies and the economic strangulation of small businesses, Wilson urged government action to destroy the trusts and restore healthy competition.

Opposing Wilson were William Howard Taft, the Republican incumbent, and Theodore Roosevelt, who came out of retirement to represent the Progressive or Bull Moose party. Taft's identification with the conservative wing of the Republican party all but eliminated his chance for victory and left Roosevelt as the main obstacle to Wilson's election. Campaigning on the platform of the New Nationalism, Roosevelt proposed an ambiguous program which accepted big business as inevitable and called for the use of federal power to regulate business and promote the welfare of the individual. Although this stand appeared to put Roosevelt and Wilson at odds on the trust question, they differed only in emphasis. Wilson called for the destruction of trusts but admitted that big business was a necessary part of economic growth. Roosevelt preferred regulation to dissolution but acknowledged that antitrust laws were needed in case regulation failed. In the absence of substantial policy differences, the election was decided on the basis of party loyalty. Roosevelt's candidacy split the Republican vote and allowed Wilson to win.

Wilson's tenure of office coincided with the peak of progressive sentiment in the United States, and his impressive legislative record reflected the public's concern with reform. With the president's support, Congress reduced the tariff, imposed an income tax, restructured the banking system, revised the antitrust laws, created the Federal Trade Commission, and approved a variety of social welfare programs. These were positive accomplishments that helped equalize the tax burden, removed some impediments to economic growth, and provided help for the victims of industrialization, but these measures were solidly conservative in that they did not change the economic or social structure. Wilson's program offered some benefit to most of the groups demanding reform while still managing to proceed with modernization. Bureaucratic values became more entrenched as governmental authority expanded into new fields and federal agencies supplied more guidance and advice to private business. Under conservative direction, the nation found ways to cope with industrialization.

American entry into World War I necessitated the further expansion of bureaucratic control, but it drew attention away from reform and ended the progressive movement. In order to supply American and Allied forces, the federal government had to mobilize the American economy. This led to the establishment of the Food Administration to regulate the production and distribution of agricultural products; the War Industries Board to supervise industrial materials, production, and labor relations; and smaller agencies to oversee fuel production and railway transportation. Order and efficiency were needed to maximize output, and the federal government assumed the responsibility for regulating and coordinating the efforts of private business. Although this was a logical extension of the prewar reform movement, the public demand for reform did not survive the war. Patriotic fervor occupied the public's attention, and the new industrial order seemed to be at bay.

Government control eased following the end of the war and business again directed the economy. The United States appeared to have passed the crisis of industrialization and reform was no longer an urgent issue.

The prosperity of the 1920s further reduced the appeal of reform. With the exception of farmers who were suffering from low prices and demanding a federal farm program, most Americans enjoyed good times and had little reason to seek more from their government. Order and stability were still high priorities among business leaders, but the focus had shifted away from the direct intervention that had characterized the prewar period. The Republican administrations of Warren G. Harding, Calvin Coolidge, and Herbert Hoover believed that business had the capacity to regulate itself and to direct economic growth along lines that would produce benefits for all of society. The government played a crucial, but limited, role in aiding business and smoothing the way for growth. Federal agencies furnished business with statistical data on economic trends, encouraged cooperation among competing businesses by helping to organize industry-wide trade associations, and used their expertise to help solve problems which business could not overcome. Social welfare legislation was at a minimum because business was expected to realize its obligation to society and spread the profits of prosperity to all. It was an era of "business progressivism" in which the government left the primary responsibility for social and economic progress to private business.

This tidy arrangement collapsed during the depression which followed the stock market crash of 1929. Public faith in business leadership disappeared as stock values plummeted, profits shrank, production decreased, and unemployment rose. Despite optimistic statements about recovery and praise for the virtues of rugged individualism, President Hoover — the leading advocate of business progressivism — was unable to develop a voluntary program to halt the decline. Mounting unemployment rates, along with a growing number of bankruptcies, the failure of many banking institutions, and the appalling toll of human suffering, finally forced Hoover to retreat from his belief in voluntary action and recognize the need for government intervention. He took steps to make federal funds available for public works projects and local relief programs, and he approved federal loans to banks, insurance companies, and railroads that were in financial danger. These efforts, however, were too limited to have much impact. Hoover left office in 1933 with the nation near total economic collapse, the people in despair and the demand for positive action growing daily.

The colossal task of leading the nation out of this economic crisis fell to Franklin D. Roosevelt. The pampered child of an economically and socially secure family, there was nothing in Roosevelt's background to incline him toward radicalism. He, like his cousin Theodore, had found it easy to support the mild reforms of the prewar period, and he had found it just as easy to accept the business progressivism of the 1920s. Franklin Roosevelt was intellectually flexible and willing to experiment with varied, sometimes contradictory, programs of action, but there were limits to his adaptability. Although he recognized as well as anyone the weaknesses and failures of corporate capitalism, he never questioned the desirability of a capitalist economy or considered any alternative. Instead, Roosevelt devoted his efforts to rebuilding and reinvigorating the ailing system.

Unlike the progressive reformers of the early twentieth century who tried to harness a rapidly expanding economy, Roosevelt faced a situation in which economic paralysis threatened the entire social system. He responded to the challenge by sponsoring an ambitious agenda of domestic legislation which sought to relieve suffering, bring about economic recovery, and reform the business system. The resulting deluge of "alphabet agencies," government regulations, and welfare programs testified to FDR's flexibility and political skill, and it led many people to believe that Roosevelt's New Deal had revolutionized American life. Suddenly the federal government was involved in the daily lives of most citizens. Government agencies began to regulate the stock exchange, guarantee labor's right to organize, administer old age pensions, subsidize farmers, provide employment for the jobless, and perform dozens of other functions that were formerly outside the realm of government responsibility. No longer, it seemed, was any facet of society beyond the scope of federal authority.

The New Deal did produce change, but those who see it as a bold departure from the past exaggerate the impact of Roosevelt's accomplishments and underestimate the continuity with earlier periods. Roosevelt certainly expanded government power, increased the influence of the executive branch, and helped relieve the suffering of millions of Americans. The New Deal recognized the needs of previously ignored groups such as organized labor and took the first steps toward assuring all Americans of a decent standard of living. However, the New Deal did not produce recovery or drastically restructure the economy. Roosevelt believed in making business responsible to the people, but he never lost his faith in capitalism. In order to save the basic components of the capitalist economy, the New Deal required business to surrender some of its traditional prerogatives and accept more regulation. It was a bitter pill for many businessmen to swallow, but it actually did little to reduce the influence or importance of business. Like the progressive movement, the New Deal was basically a conservative response to crisis.

The major significance of the New Deal is that it modified the rules under which the economic system operated and completed the process of modernization that had begun during the Progressive Era. The new middle class of the prewar years had never challenged the domination of corporate capitalism and had been content with using a minimum of government regulation to achieve the order and stability that the private sector could not supply. The economic crisis of the 1930s, however, demonstrated that a complex industrial state could not rely solely upon the good sense and altruism of business to assure progress. Business could not be allowed the luxury of employing government power only for selfish advantage nor could it continue to exclude non-business groups from sharing the power and benefits. If the modern state was to function smoothly and continue its development, the bureaucratic values of order, stability, predictability, and uniformity had to be applied across the board. Roosevelt's New Deal legislation did this by defining the role of business, labor, and government and supervising their interaction.

By greatly expanding government regulation, institutionalizing the concept of the welfare state, and recognizing non-business groups, the New Deal tried to realize the goal of an integrated industrial state. It did not achieve complete success, but it established ground rules that remain unchallenged. Although there have been a variety of reform programs and changes since World War II, they have done little more than expand on the approach and policies of Roosevelt and the New Deal. Despite some sacrifice of individualism and independent action, the United States has managed to meet the challenge of industrialization with conservative reforms that have preserved the capitalist economy and not upset the social structure.

SUGGESTED READINGS

The student interested in pursuing the topic of twentieth century reform should first consult the survey accounts. William L. O'Neill, *The Progressive Years: America Comes of Age* (1975) provides a good introduction to the progressive era but should be supplemented with Samuel P. Hays, *The Response to Industrialism, 1885-1914* (1957) and Robert H. Wiebe, *The Search for Order, 1877-1920* (1967). The conservative character of progressivism is discussed at length in Gabriel Kolko, *The Triumph of Conservatism: A Reinterpretation of American History, 1900-1916* (1963): James Weinstein, *The Corporate Ideal in the Liberal State, 1900-1918* (1968); Robert H. Wiebe, *Businessmen and Reform: A Study of the Progressive Movement* (1962). A different interpretation can be found in George E. Mowry, *The Era of Theodore Roosevelt* (1958) and Richard Hofstadter, *The Age of Reform* (1955). The best treatment of the 1920s is Joan Hoff Wilson, *Herbert Hoover: Forgotten Progressive* (1975), but a more traditional view is Arthur S. Link, "Whatever Happened to the Progressive Movement in the 1920s?," *American Historical Review*, 64 (July, 1959). The basic account of the New Deal is William E. Leuchtenburg, *Franklin D. Roosevelt and the New Deal* (1963), a balanced assessment of FDR's accomplishments. The conservative nature of New Deal reform is illuminated in Barton J. Bernstein, "The New Deal: The Conservative Achievements of Liberal Reform," in Bernstein, ed., *Towards a New Past: Dissenting Essays in American History* (1968) and Paul Conkin, *The New Deal* (1967). Although I disagree with some of his conclusions, the essays on Theodore Roosevelt, Herbert Hoover, and Franklin Roosevelt in Richard Hofstadter, *The American Political Tradition and the Men Who Made It* (1948) contain valuable insights into the entire period and merit close study.

Interrupting the Ceremony. (Chicago Tribune)

CHAPTER SIX

The American Response To Two World Wars

FRANK W. ABBOTT

War, whenever and wherever it touched the American people, stirred a jumble of responses. Most Americans, like Franklin Delano Roosevelt, could say they genuinely hated war. But a nation forged in war and proud of its martial accomplishments could not deny the compelling heritage of victory. It mattered not that the Americans did not always win, they believed they always did. War brought them good. It brought them independence; it brought them pride; it brought them territory; it brought them limited reform; it brought them respect. It took away fathers, brothers, husbands, and sons who never returned or who returned maimed beyond belief. The Americans overcame their grief with a drink for the living, a toast for the dead, and a once annual nod to the crippled, but they would not turn away from the conflict. If the Americans hated war, they welcomed the reminiscence of past glory and comradeship.

The Americans did not want war. At least, the Americans did not believe that they wanted war. Neither in 1917 nor in 1941, did Americans believe that their actions constituted sufficient cause for other nations to make war on the United States. The American people were a peaceful people. "I'm a peaceable fellow," "Wild Bill" Elliott intoned in a dozen Republic "B" movies popular during the 1940s and early 1950s. "I'm a peaceable fellow" he would say as he drew his six-gun and blasted the bad guys. So, too, were the Americans "peaceable fellows." Woodrow Wilson, a philosophic pacifist, would finally resort to war because as he told Congress in his war message, "right is more precious than peace." So, too, would war-hater Franklin Roosevelt call for war in 1941 because it had been forced upon him. Americans sought, in their minds, only peace.

In the twentieth century, the United States in its search for peace fought two major conflicts rightly called "world wars." Though both wars occurred within a twenty-five year span, they came to different nations. World War I, beginning for the world in 1914 and for the United States in 1917, involved a nation passing through the metamorphosis from rural to urban. In 1917, the United States was still a rural nation. The American heritage and value system drew upon the rural roots. It upheld the values of independence and self-sufficiency. It distrusted things alien to the culture, and it saw no reason why the nation should not have its own way in affairs.

The urban values had not yet reached a position to challenge the rural society, but those urban values had begun to pose alternatives. The new values stressed the concepts of interdependence and group action for survival. Each group shared an allegiance to the concept of the free man, but for each, the definition differed.

The rural value held that the free man existed as an unfettered entity, able to do as he desired with few restraints. Limits placed upon the freedom of action reduced the sovereignty of the individual, and it took very few restraints to turn a free man into a slave. The urban values, conversely, accepted limitations on the freedom of action as a necessary part of group activity. While both groups would stress the primacy of the individual over the group, the urban value system tended to use group activity with greater frequency to achieve a stable society. Along with the higher frequency of group action went recognition of the concept that individual wishes had sometimes to be subordinated to the group so that all would survive. "Root, hog, or die" was giving way.

By 1941, the United States was an urban nation. The census of 1920 documented that fact. The rural values which dominated 1914 had not disappeared, but they no longer had exclusive control of the society. The nation, suffering under the grievous deprivation of the Great Depression, adopted more and more group responses to the problems posed by economic dislocation. While the more radical group activities such as Rexford Tugwell's collective farm programs met widespread disapproval, moderate collective activity such as social welfare became a standard response. David Lilienthal talked of the "web of nature" as having been his guide in developing the Tennessee Valley Authority. By that, Lilienthal meant the interrelatedness of man, land, and life in the Tennessee Valley. The "web" spread from Tennessee to the nation. Thus, as the world entered the Second World War, collective action became more acceptable to the United States. By a narrow margin, such programs as lend-lease met United States approval.

This essay concerns the progress of that change as it affected foreign policy and as it stemmed from the impact of the first war upon the society.

World War I broke over a stunned world in August 1914, more the result of misinformation, misperception, and misdirection than calculated design. The assassination of the Austrian Archduke Franz Ferdinand resulted in an Austrian ultimatum to Serbia who appealed to Russia for support which Russia granted while mobilizing her armies which prompted German mobilization that brought French mobilization that caused the German implementation of the von Schlieffen plan which included invasion of France through Belgium bringing Great Britain into the war because of her guarantees of Belgium neutrality (if that sentence seems confusing, think of how the events confused everyone at the time).

For the Americans, the war evoked great horror. Enlightened opinion had held that war on such a scale could not take place. The development of a network of trade relationships made it impossible for those nations to war on each other. The trading nations might compete fiercely for protected spheres of influence, but they needed each other's goods too much to deprive their economies through war. Furthermore, the long period of world peace — it had been one hundred years since Napoleon's armies had been defeated — convinced many people that peace was the norm. Granting the numerous localized conflicts since 1814, war appeared to be a modern aberration of human conduct. Social Darwinism, very much in vogue among the educated class of 1914, buttressed the feeling that war was outmoded by suggesting an explanation for the disappearance of war. Mankind had risen above its earlier animal instincts for conflict. So, too, did the twenty years preceding the war suggest a similar conclusion. Europe had remained in constant turmoil during those two decades with each convolution of the geopolitical map of Europe threatening war. Each year, it seemed, had a crisis which brought the world to the brink of war. From the Agadir Crisis, to the First and Second Bosnian Wars, to the several Moroccan Crises, Europe seemed on the verge of explosion. Each time, the crisis passed. War did not come; and to the optimist, this was a sign that war would never occur. Nevertheless, in August 1914, the improbable war began.

Woodrow Wilson personified the American shock and revulsion with the war issuing a Neutrality Proclamation calling upon the American people to be neutral in "thought and deed." As later scholars judged, the request demanded more than many Americans, particularly first and second generation immigrants, could give. Yet, the proclamation reflected the traditional American values that stretched back to 1793. The United States could stand alone, it needed neither Europe nor the world. Consequently, it should not dabble in the world's troubles. Reality posed a different set of guidelines.

As it had long acted, the United States played the role of the leading neutral carrier. Neutrality allowed the nation to enjoy the benefits of continued commerce with all nations including the belligerents. But continued trade meant a continued American presence in the war zone, and that presence precluded noninvolvement. The war trade, in fact, pulled the United States out of a minor recession in 1914 and insured general prosperity for the nation. The myth of American self-sufficiency collided with the necessity of American participation in the neutral trade.

The war-enforced reality did not bring instant reevaluation of the American position. The people continued to hope that the war would pass them by. The feelings grew more intense as the new technology began to play an active part in the war. To a generation accustomed to peace, the war seemed particularly destructive. On the land, the new armored tanks made an appearance spewing death. Rifles did not stop these products of the motor age. Neither did rifles help against the fragile airplanes which began mid-way through the war to take a ground support role through strafing and bombing. Beyond these mobile destroyers, two new weapons, the machine gun and poison gas, also placed the man in the trenches in an exposed and deadly position.

The machine gun was not, strictly speaking, a new weapon. There had been automatic firing weapons prior to the war; rather the machine gun represented a second generation rapid firing weapon. As such, it far outstripped the ability of the generals to find ways around it. Strategically placed a machine gun company could hold off a division, several machine gun companies could hold off an army. Getting there "firstest with the mostest" no longer guaranteed victory. Mass charges, such as those by the Germans at Verdun, resulted not in victory, but in mass death, for the Germans lost a quarter of a million men attacking this heavily defended French position in 1916.

A soldier could hide from the tank, the airplane, or the machine gun if he chose his position carefully, stayed down, and did not attack. In 1915, the Germans introduced a new weapon which made of all those standards for protection obsolete — poison gas. Lobbed by artillery, the chlorine gas canisters ruptured and a greenish haze spread across the battlefield bringing death to those who inhaled it. Soon both sides were preparing assaults by laying down a deadly fog before their troops, and the chemical warfare sections of all armies worked at developing newer and more effective gases. Mustard gas left hundred of thousands of soldiers with badly burned bodies and abscessed lungs, for the gas burned whatever it touched. Gas masks could help against chlorine gas, it would protect the lungs, but a gas mask in a mustard gas attack protected only the eyes, nose, and throat. Any part of the body which was not covered received a very painful burn which would incapacitate the soldier. There was no longer a place to hide.

The use of these new weapons shocked and stunned Americans. Civilized nations who had outgrown the need to make war had now found new ways to make war more deadly than ever before. Each day the casualty lists grew longer and longer as a generation of European men marched to extinction. Americans thanked God, George Washington, and Woodrow Wilson that those lists contained few Americans. But the Americans remained in the war zone, and occasionally at first, and then more often, the lists carried the names of a few unlucky Americans who were victims of one additional weapon, the submarine.

Leon C. Thrasher was the first. Thrasher had sailed on the *Falaba*, and he died when a German U-boat torpedoed the ship. The torpedoing of the *Lusitania* in February 1915, caused the death of 128 Americans. The *Lusitania* brought an angry American reaction to the submarine as a weapon. The submarine attacked without warning and without following the customary rules of warfare. Furthermore, the submarine brought death at sea, and such death has always exercised a peculiar horror for Americans because it deprived the land-conscious Americans of a final resting place in a plot of ground. Thus, the submarine, which brought this most horrible of deaths, called forth the base values of the American culture and drove the nation to the final crisis.

Wilson responded to the submarine by warning the Germans to stop the unprovoked attacks on neutral vessels. The sinking of the *Lusitania* prompted an even stronger note in which Wilson, typing the first draft on his own typewriter, warned Germany that it would be held in "strict accountability" for lives lost. The United States, by holding to its root values, had begun to draw the final line. The torpedoing of the French liner *Sussex* in March 1916, elicited a threat that continued submarine attacks would force the United States to break off relations with Germany, an action widely interpreted as being preparatory to war.

That *Sussex* warning brought about an intense struggle inside the German high command between the military and the civilian sections. The civilians won, and Germany issued the required promise to end unrestricted submarine warfare. For one year that pledge held.

Wilson used the time to seek a negotiated peace which he hoped would prevent the United States from entering the war. While he searched, the American people reelected him, by a very narrow margin. The Democratic party had used the peace issue in the campaign, reminding the voters that Wilson had "kept us out of war," while the Republican candidate, Charles Evans Hughes was saddled with the bellicose Theodore Roosevelt.

Wilson had not, of course, kept the United States out of war. He had taken a forceful stand that left the decision of American entry into the war in the hands of Germany. While Wilson attempted to bring a negotiated peace in the fall of 1916, Germany underwent another intense internal debate that ended in a victory of the military wing of the government. On January 31, 1917, Count Bernstorff, the German Ambassador, handed two notes to the United States. The first stated that Germany would not come to any peace conference called by the United States; the second announced that on February 1, 1917, Germany would reopen unrestricted submarine warfare. Wilson did not act preemptively, but within a few weeks German submarine sinkings of merchant ships prompted Wilson to ask for a declaration of war. The war, he said to Congress, would be a war to "make the world safe for democracy."

Values did not change as the United States entered the war. The rural desire for independence and freedom of action stayed atop the political scene. The United States became not an "ally" of France and Great Britain, but an "Associated Power." In France, General John Pershing, commander of the American Expeditionary Force, held out for a separate command sector rather than allowing American troops to be piecemealed into the line to shore up British and French troops. The Allied Powers, needing desperately to acquire the material wealth which the United States had in abundance, found that America would supply all the Allies' needs for a price. As a result, the Europeans went deeply into debt to the United States to acquire the supplies.

At home, urban values grew as American participation in the war increased. Society became regimented. Big business got the call to produce more goods; the government urged the people to sacrifice food, coal, and money for the war; a massive conscription program went into effect with only momentary delay and little effective opposition. Within months, rather than the year Germany had estimated, the United States was on its way "Over There."

Toleration, which is a part of the urban value scheme, did not accompany the regimentation. Little Lou Gehrig found himself surrounded by bully boys on the streets of New York because of his German name. Kansas prohibited the teaching of the German language. Homburg Steak had its name changed to the more English sounding "Salisbury Steak." Those who opposed the war on philosophic grounds such as the Socialist leader Eugene V. Debs found themselves in jail for violating the Espionage Act. Rural values still dominated the day.

Rural as they might be, the American people rallied to urban battle cries. Wilson in his war message had justified the war as an effort by the democracies to quell the power of autocracy. The war aims made public by Wilson in the Fourteen Points Address in January 1918, reflected urban values when it called for a general association of nations to preserve peace in the postwar world. During the war, the public supported these urban values, in part because they were cloaked in the rhetoric of rural America. Without realizing it, the people had supported a cause that meant drastic change. When the threat ended, the change became clearer, and the fight over the acceptance of Treaty of Versailles illustrated the two views.

The Treaty of Versailles which came out of the Paris Peace Conference in 1919 reflected many points of view. The French wanted revenge and reassurance; they obtained the former without the latter. The British wanted a peace that justified their sacrifice and protected their interests; they secured the latter without the former. The Italians wanted territory and more territory; they gained very little. The Americans wanted a peace without victory; they received both a peace and victory, then rejected the settlement.

The treaty fight in the Senate concerned itself little with either peace or victory. Rather it centered on the role the United States would play in the postwar world. Supporters of the treaty grouped themselves behind the urban values which it represented. They promoted the Covenant of the League of Nations because it promised an interdependent world in which the United States would be a joint participant. They criticized those sections of the treaty which worked against those aims — particularly they protested the "war guilt" clause, the reparations agreements, and the avoidance of self-determination in dealing with many of the colonial problems. The opponents of the treaty fought what they saw to be an abandonment of the American principle of freedom of action. If it joined the League of Nations, the United States would run the risk of being forced to let other nations decide what actions were acceptable. "We are not an internationalist bawdy house," wrote one opponent, "nor an anarchist cafe." Another opponent succinctly summed up with moving rhetoric,

> We believe the United States will not consent to any super-sovereignty in any territory where flies the Stars and Stripes. . . . We can give a satisfactory account of ourselves to civilization, not to a society composed of governments.

In the end, the rural values triumphed. Historians would later engage in an effort to affix blame for the rejection of the treaty by the Senate. Pro-Wilson scholars would blame Henry Cabot Lodge — and most of the writers on the topic were pro-Wilson. One pro-Wilsonian writing during World War II, Thomas A. Bailey, would place the responsibility elsewhere. The defeat of the treaty was, he wrote, the "supreme infanticide." Wilson had killed his own offspring. But the treaty failed more nearly because, without the heat of wartime emotion, the rural-oriented American nation could not accept urban values.

The years between the wars saw an increasing conflict between the rural and urban values in both domestic and foreign affairs. Domestically, the nation divided over prohibition, immigration, Sacco and Vanzetti, government action to relieve suffering in the private sector, and a dozen issues along urban/rural lines. Historians have chronicled these splits in great detail. In foreign affairs, this same urban/rural split played a similar role which has engendered less study. The disillusionment which accompanied the end of the war hid some of the division as both groups tended to feel less at home in the disorganized postwar world. But the issues, many war-related, which arose brought an urban/rural division.

In the twenties, the rural values continued to dominate policy. The United States sought self-sufficiency and freedom of action. It wanted no responsibility for the postwar settlement, but it sought no withdrawal from affairs. The rhetoric of isolation might remain, but even those most associated with the term advocated an American presence in the world. The war taught that lesson well.

Ending the war illustrated the new position. By rejecting the Treaty of Versailles, the United States left itself still at war, officially, with Germany. The Congress repealed the war declaration, and the State Department negotiated a separate peace treaty which reserved for the United States all the rights which it might have enjoyed had it approved the Treaty of Versailles, but specifically renounced any American intention to play a role in enforcing that treaty. The United States adopted a similar position toward the Allied Powers.

The war did great damage to the European economies. France and England suffered particularly because their once dominant creditor position had eroded, and their industry, on a war footing for four years, could not make the peacetime conversion without surplus capital. That capital was not available except from increased trade or through German reparations. Moreover, the United States insisted that the Allies begin paying back the large American loans made during the war, a demand which siphoned off needed capital. Germany, too, suffered from the war. The continued blockade had reduced many Germans to starvation, and the terrible demands of the war effort had left German industry depleted. The Germans, too, needed capital to regenerate prosperity. But their surplus capital, and much that was not surplus, went to the Allies to make the reparation payments demanded by the Treaty of Versailles. On several occasions the Allies offered to scale down the reparations bill presented Germany, if the United States would make similar reductions in the war debts. Consistently, the United States refused to consider any adjustment, all the while arguing on behalf of Germany that the reparations bill was too high. Two Americans, Charles Dawes and Owen Young, participated in commissions which were established to reorganize the German economic system and the payback schedule. Nevertheless, the United States refused to accept any connection between German reparations and Allied war debts. Instead, the United States warned Europe that it must always consider American interests in any settlement, but that it must not expect any American assistance in enforcing any agreements.

Trade issues showed a similar American position. The European economies needed to have increased trade if they were to recover from the war. The United States as the only creditor nation in the postwar period, and as the leading industrial nation provided the only real market for those European goods. But the return of Republican Normalcy meant a return to traditional tariff policies. President Warren Harding once explained to journalist Bruce Bliven that the United States needed a "high protective tariff to help the struggling industries of Europe." The high tariffs enacted — the Emergency Tariff in 1921, the Fordney-McCumber Tariff in 1922, and the Smoot-Hawley Tariff in 1930 — did little except stifle world trade. Prior to the signing of the Smoot-Hawley Tariff, two hundred members of the American Economic Association protested the legislation to President Herbert Hoover on the grounds that it would cause reprisals which would bring international trade to a standstill. Hoover chose to reject the arguments of the economists and signed the bill saying that it would aid in general economic recovery. As the economists had predicted, reprisals from Europe accompanied the implementation of the bill, and American industry, which had for many years produced more than the American market could absorb, found its foreign markets drying up. It helped the nation down the road to depression.

The rural dominance in policy appeared in the efforts at world peace in the decade as well. Both sides believed that world peace was considerably better than world war, and both believed that efforts toward that end were necessary. Some attempts did occur. In 1921, the United States called for an international conference on disarmament, and the resulting Washington Naval Conference did bring reduction in the size and number of naval vessels. Though the major agreement, the Five Power Treaty, did result in the destruction of several ships and a ten year moratorium on battleship construction, the United States had no enforcement provision written into the treaty. Enforcement provisions, as the nation knew, would limit the freedom of action. The Kellog-Briand Pact of 1927, the treaty which "outlawed war as an instrument of national policy," also contained no enforcement provision. The United States devised the plan that way. France had made the original treaty suggestion because it wanted to tie the United States morally to the defense of France. Secretary of State Frank Kellogg threw the treaty negotiations open to all the world so that none would bear responsibility. Both rural forces and urban forces regarded the treaty as a farce.

Throughout the decade, the urban forces showed increasing strength. In negotiations with Mexico on behalf of oil interests, J. Rueben Clark argued forcefully for American recognition of the rights of other nations to control their resources. In the struggle over American membership in the World Court, the war debt fight, and the tariff fight, the urban position of an interdependent world and the necessity of group action made each rural triumph more costly. In the thirties, the urban position began to assert itself.

The rise of the fascist dictators in Italy and Germany had, by the 1930s, begun to pose a threat to world peace. Italy under Mussolini made strident efforts to acquire a new Roman Empire. After some early gains in the Mediterranean area, Italy began to look farther south around Somaliland, her African colony. Hitler, beginning in the mid-1930s, led Germany through a steady period of remilitarization and pressure on neighboring areas. Both nations threatened the status quo in Europe.

Italy struck first. In October 1935, Italian mechanized units invaded Ethiopia. The attack came without surprise. As early as February, observers had predicted an October invasion because the rainy season would have ended and the ground would be dry enough for motorized operation. The invasion succeeded rapidly. Ethiopian troops, many armed only with spears, proved no match for the Italian machine guns. Emperor Haile Selassie flew to Geneva where he called upon the League of Nations to impose sanctions upon Italy to save his country. The League responded hesitatingly watching for an American response to the aggression.

The United States had already taken action. Concerned that the Italian invasion might develop into a general war, the Congress passed in August the first Neutrality Act. The law required the President upon finding that a state of war existed to prohibit munitions shipment to belligerents and to prohibit Americans from sailing in a war zone except at their own risk. This act and the other acts which followed in 1936, 1937, and 1939 have often been described as the triumph of isolation. The legislation, which stemmed from fear of involvement in a second war and passed because the rural segments believed the legislation would preserve American freedom of action, also enjoyed support from those with urban values. The urban support stemmed from a hope that the United States could enter the interdependent world through the side door. Promises that the United States would not send arms to belligerents would reenforce League sanctions on aggressors. Thus, the argument went, the United States would be a part, albeit indirectly, of the interdependent League action.

The neutrality laws failed to achieve the urban purpose. When the first act expired in 1936, the urban elements campaigned without success against renewal. Later neutrality legislation added a ban on loans to belligerents while making the munitions and travel prohibitions permanent. The acts intended to maintain freedom of action actually limited the American options. As the world marched closer to war, the laws prevented the United States from acting to head off the calamity. By 1939, the world had opted for battle a second time to settle conflict.

The war came to the United States in stages. First, Europe went to war, and the United States stayed aloof from the conflict. With the fall of France in June 1940, American involvement stepped up. The neutrality acts were reinterpreted to allow belligerents to purchase supplies in the United States if they paid for the material in cash and shipped the goods in non-American bottoms ("cash and carry"). By the fall of 1940, Britain had exhausted her money. Winston Churchill appealed to Roosevelt for assistance, and Roosevelt's response typified the urban value. The program, called lend-lease, promised that the United States would lend or lease to the British such goods as she might require to fight the war. At the conclusion of hostilities, Britain would either return the goods or make payments in kind. Roosevelt explained the program with the analogy of a man loaning a garden hose to a neighbor whose house was on fire. When the fire was out, the neighbor could return or replace the hose. A bitter fight over lend-lease followed within the Congress, but the bill passed.

From early 1941 through December, the United States moved more deeply into the conflict. Joint British-American staff conferences on the deployment of American troops occurred through March; American naval vessels began convoying supplies as far as Iceland; American destroyers patrolled the North Atlantic tracking German submarines. By the fall, the United States was in an undeclared naval war with Germany.

Formal hostilities arrived from another quarter of the world. While the government had concentrated its attention on the coming war with Germany, relations with Japan deteriorated as the United States opposed Japanese aggression in

China. On December 7, 1941, the Japanese launched a surprise attack on the United States naval base at Pearl Harbor. The following day Franklin Roosevelt asked for and received with only one dissenting vote a declaration of war on Japan.[1] Two days later Italy and Germany declared war on the United States, and the United States reciprocated.

Americans, genuinely shocked by the surprise attack, turned determinedly to waging war. The bitter policy divisions within the nation healed quickly, and the nation determined to gain revenge on the Japanese and to destroy the fascists. Behind much of the preparation for war went an equal determination to avoid the mistakes of the first conflict. Big business received the call for war material, but with it went an excess profits tax. Citizens were asked to sacrifice luxury for the war, but with sacrifice went tax reform and price controls to stifle inflation. The government refused to propagandize the war as it had World War I. Toleration of divergent opinion did not appear, but, except in the case of the Japanese, little concentrated suppression occurred. The second war came to an urban nation.

This time around, the Americans participated on an interdependent basis. The United States became an allied power under the terms of the Atlantic Charter. Its forces fought side by side with soldiers of all the United Nations in integrated commands. Allies who needed material found the American storehouse open. The fighting was done in the spirit of a nation which recognized the interdependence of all nations in the common struggle for peace.

Committed to avoiding the mistakes made in fighting World War I, the Americans also committed themselves to avoiding the mistakes of the peace. The urban values now stood triumphant. A general association of nations now called the United Nations came about as a separate entity and gained Senate approval. Texas Senator Tom Connally told recalcitrant Senators,

> Many representatives of foreign nations are still doubtful as to what the vote on the Charter will be here in the Senate. They remember 1919. They know how the League of Nations was slaughtered here on the floor. Can you not still see the blood?

---

[1] It is interesting to note that the one dissenting vote cast in 1941 came from Jeanette Rankin, who served two terms in Congress, one in 1917-1918, and one 1941-1942. A pacifist, she voted against American participation in World I and World War II, the only person to have that distinction.

Twentieth Century Fox spent several million dollars making a biography of Woodrow Wilson which asserted in every frame that had the nation accepted the League in 1919, World War II would not have occurred. The charter of the United Nations passed the Senate eighty-nine to two.

When in the postwar period, the European economies, never fully recovered from the first war, collapsed again, the United States responded with an urban program. To hasten rehabilitation, the United States proposed the Marshall Plan which poured seventeen billion dollars into European recovery. It represented an urban recognition that the United States needed a prosperous world if it would remain prosperous as well.

To gain sufficient votes to enact the Marshall Plan, the Truman administration sold the program as a part of the needed effort to contain the Soviet Union. Gradually, in the postwar world the center focus of American policy became the struggle with the Soviet Union. That struggle took the United States away from the truly interdependent philosophy which had emerged during the war, but the commitment to that philosophy changed the nature of the American response. No longer did the United States seek to avoid the responsibility for enforcing the postwar settlements. Actively, even eagerly, the United States sought not just a role, but the dominant role in enforcing that settlement. It acted ahead of rather than with the world. It drew back from, as the phrase went in the discussion of multilateral control of atomic weapons in NATO, "too many fingers on the trigger." Yet, throughout, it spoke in urban terms.

War, when it came, stirred many responses. To the rural nation of 1919, it called forth rural values of independence which clashed with the challenge of urban interdependence. The Second World War provided the catalyst which insured the success of that interdependent philosophy. The struggle between rural and urban America ended, and new lights governed United States policy.

SUGGESTED READINGS

The literature on war and its impact on American society is, as one might expect, quite extensive. A useful compilation of reading by a wide variety of historians on war is Keith L. Nelson, ed., *The Impact of War on American Life* (1971).

The urban/rural split as it affected domestic policy is also extensive. One of the best short surveys which treats the interwar years from this perspective is George Mowry, *The Urban Nation* (1965).

Ernest R. May, *The World War and American Isolation* (1959) is among the best recent examinations of American entry into World War I. For Wilson's overall policy goals, however, N. Gordon Levin, *Woodrow Wilson and World Politics* (1968) is an excellent interpretation. Arthur S. Link, *Wilson the Diplomatist* (1956) remains the best general introduction to Wilsonian diplomacy in action. The Peace Conference is the subject of numerous surveys. Thomas A. Bailey, *Woodrow Wilson and the Lost Peace* (1944) is among the most readable, while Arno J. Mayer, *Politics and Diplomacy of Peacemaking* (1967) is a provocative New Left interpretation. Thomas A. Bailey, *Woodrow Wilson and the Great Betrayal* (1945) is the standard study of the fight over the Treaty of Versailles in the Senate, but it should be supplemented with Ralph Stone, *The Irreconcilables* (1970).

There have been few good surveys of foreign policy between the war, but an excellent general introduction is Selig Adler, *The Isolationist Impulse* (1957). For other events of the period, monographs provide the best source. On the Washington Naval Conference and disarmament, Raymond L. Buell, *The Washington Naval Conference* (1922) is old but still valuable. John C. Vinson, *The Parchment Peace* (1955) is a more recent study of the same topic. The best study of the Kellogg-Briand Pact is Robert Ferrell, *Peace in Their Time* (1952). Recent work in the twenties has indicated the changes that were taking place in the State Department. See particularly N. Stephen Kane, "Corporate Power and Foreign Policy: Efforts of the Oil Companies to Influence American Relations with Mexico, 1921-1928," *Diplomatic History*, 1 (Spring, 1977).

The development of the Neutrality Acts and information on voting patterns can best be found in Robert Divine, *The Illusion of Neutrality* (1962). For American entry into World War II, a useful general survey is Robert Divine, *The Reluctant Belligerent* (1965), while the classic longer study is William Langer and S. E. Gleason, *The Challenge to Isolation, 1937-1940* (1952) and the continuation in *The Undeclared War, 1940-1941* (1953) by the same authors. Opponents of American intervention in

World War II can be studied in Wayne S. Cole, *America First* (1953). The homefront is covered by John M. Blum, *V was for Victory* (1976). For wartime diplomacy, Gaddis Smith, *American Diplomacy during the Second World War* (1965) is a useful general survey, while Gabriel Kolko, *The Politics of War* (1968) provides a New Left interpretation of the development of American postwar policy. Military aspects are covered in A. Russell Buchannan, *The United States and World War II* (2 volumes, 1964). The study of American acceptance of the United Nations is best dealt with in Robert Divine, *Second Chance: The Triumph of Internationalism During the Second World War* (1967).

For postwar developments, the best short survey is Norman Graebner, *Cold War Diplomacy* (2nd edition 1977), but see Louis Halle, *The Cold War as History* (1968) for an excellent interpretative study. Other changes in American policy can be studied in Stephen Ambrose, *Rise to Globalism* (1972), and Simon Serfaty, *The Elusive Enemy* (1972). See also the bibliographic essay at the conclusion of Professor MacDonald's essay.

ATOMIC BLAST: The second atomic bomb was exploded on Nagasaki 9 August 1945. (U.S. Air Force Photo)

CHAPTER SEVEN

American Foreign Policy Since 1945

WILLIAM W. MACDONALD

World War II had a profound impact upon American society because it accelerated social, political and economic trends already apparent and stimulated change, for good or evil, that had not seemed possible even in the turbulent period of the Depression. The war brought great prosperity to millions of Americans, ended the greatest economic catastrophe the nation had ever known, and liberated many women by providing job opportunities previously denied them. The immense cost of fighting World War II, together with full employment and progressive tax legislation, resulted in a more equitable redistribution of wealth and, at the same time, offered many Americans, particularly those in the minority groups, college educations and access to positions of power previously barred to them. The war had a significant influence in hastening the industrialization of the West and South, in continuing the reshuffling of large numbers of American families from the country to the cities, and in providing marked advances, however slow and tortuous, for black Americans. World War II, moreover, had destroyed Fascism, and the technological advances stimulated by the necessities of defeating Germany and Japan, seemed to promise a better world as well as a more peaceful one. It was these factors that prompted many Americans to view the war not only as a seminal event in the history of America, but also as an actual benefit to mankind, especially Americans.

The most overpowering factor of World War II upon American society, however, was in the war's influence in changing, shaping and directing American foreign policy. The Allied defeat of the Axis powers left the United States endowed with a power, prestige, and mission unparalleled in her history, for the American victories in Europe and Asia had catapulted the U.S. into a preeminent position in world affairs and shattered, probably beyond redemption, the traditional American policy of isolationism, which had been enshrined as an article of faith by American foreign policymakers since George Washington. The war not only changed the direction of American foreign policy but also transformed the conduct of American diplomacy, for unlike World War I, the American entry into World War II was essentially an acute response to changes in the balance of power, and American leadership during and after the war made isolationism an impossibility. With the vivid memories of 1919 to guide it, the America of 1945 was at last prepared to assume the burdens of responsibilities of world leadership. This was essentially the policy of President Roosevelt who, though he often condemned the term "power politics," urged Americans willingly to accept the duty of world leadership to avoid another world war. It was the policy of Wendell Wilkie, Roosevelt's Republican opponent for president in 1940, whose famous and influential book *One World* (1943) passionately promoted America's involvement in world politics. These internationalist, as opposed to isolationist, hopes found expression in the Connally Resolution of 1943, in which the U.S. Senate resolved that the U.S. join "with free and sovereign nations in the establishment and maintenance of international authority with power to prevent aggression and to preserve the peace of the world." Isolationism, even as a term, had disappeared into the atomic waste of Hiroshima; and yet, the impact of the disappearance of isolationism was surely not apparent to the American people in 1945.

The U.S. entered the postwar era determined not to repeat the mistakes in judgment made after World War I. Never again, or so it seemed, would Americans withdraw from the world in a fashion that might sow the seeds for World War III. Indeed, the war ended with the U.S. firmly entrenched in the United Nations and with most Americans expecting the Allied Alliance to remain intact and the "five policemen" (U.S., Russia, China,

France and England) of the Security Council to maintain the peace of the world by patrolling the behavior of the smaller, more belligerent nations. The apparently successful wartime diplomatic negotiations between Roosevelt, Sir Winston Churchill, the British Prime Minister, and Joseph Stalin, the Russian dictator, encouraged many Americans to hope that Communist Russia had abandoned her traditional revolutionary Marxist ideology of permanent hostility to world capitalism and would instead cooperate with the western capitalist democracies to rebuild a shattered world.

Events in Europe and Asia quickly made a mockery of these fallacious hopes. The Allied victory had raised a new and greater menace to America's international role in world affairs, for the enormous destruction and dislocations of World War II had all but destroyed any sense of predictability in world affairs. Stability in Europe and the Far East had collapsed. Pieces of the old French, British and Dutch empires in Africa and Asia floated free on a tide of revolutionary nationalism. The defeat of Germany, Italy and Japan, and the exhaustion of two of the victors, England and France, had brought massive shifts in the international balance of power. The rapid extension of Soviet control over most of Eastern Europe, the fall of China to the Red Chinese under Mao Tse-Tung, and the American action and reaction to those events precipitated an intense struggle between the U.S. and the Soviet Union which dominated international affairs for three decades.

Even the form of the struggle was unprecedented in world history, for more than just national interests divided the two major super powers. Conflicting ideological ideas and institutions locked the two systems into certain hostility, forcing much of the world into the emerging pattern of ideological camps, with names like "the free world" and the "non-free world." The United States and the Soviet Union each believed that the very safety, the very existence, of its respective cultures and civilizations required that its institutions and policies be exported to the rest of the world. A very complicated struggle over abstractions and national interests ensued that traditional diplomacy apparently could not resolve. The result of all these factors was the Cold War, a pivotal event in American history that is still shaping, directing and influencing all aspects of American life. There is little doubt that the Cold War was/is a tapestry against which all facets of American domestic and foreign affairs have to contend and must be measured.

The Grand Alliance against the Axis (but particularly against the Nazis) was a marriage of military convenience that dissolved when the common enemy was defeated. Most American historians now argue that President Roosevelt had assumed that the U.S. would have to acquiesce to some inevitable expansion of Soviet Russia's influence in Eastern Europe after the end of World War II because the Russian armies had occupied most of that area. Roosevelt was a confirmed "spheres-of-influence" president, who readily accepted the rather realistic division of the world into areas of Great Power influence. This was, Roosevelt concluded, the price the U.S. and its western allies had to pay for Russia's help in defeating Hitler and for resurrecting a shattered balance of power that had all but disappeared. This policy of "accommodation" of the Soviet Union, a policy that essentially conceded to the Russians what they would have demanded anyway, was based upon Roosevelt's acute reading of Russia's quest for security. The Soviet Union, which had suffered incredible damage from World War II, had witnessed German armies twice within a generation launch an invasion of Russia through Poland and the other Eastern European states. Communist Russia, historically profoundly suspicious of western democracies' motives toward the Soviet Union, often with good cause, had developed a paranoid mentality toward the capitalist nations of the world. After the Soviets had expelled the Nazis from Russia and their armies had conquered most of Eastern Europe, Stalin naturally desired and demanded security for his country, which meant, in cold, cynical language, security against Germany, "friendly" governments on the borders of Russia, massive American loans to rebuild the shattered Russian economy and, Russia's central post-World War II foreign policy goal, a Soviet Union free from external menace.

Most of these postwar problems had been discussed and debated, but not settled, at various meetings between the Allies during the war, the most famous and pivotal meeting being the Yalta Conference in February, 1945. At Yalta American hopes for a peaceful world reached their zenith, for as Harry Hopkins wrote,

We really believed in our hearts that this was the dawn of the new day we had been praying for and talking about for so many years. We were absolutely certain that we had won the first great victory of the peace. . .

But Yalta did not bring peace; nor did it solve the problem of Poland, "friendly" governments to Russia in Eastern Europe, or the problem of Germany. It did not alleviate Soviet suspicions of the motives of the capitalist nations of the West; instead, it increased tensions. The failure to resolve all these postwar problems helped to create the dawn of the Cold War.

Harry S. Truman, who had been badly informed about American foreign policy during his tenure as Vice-President, inherited all of Roosevelt's foreign affair problems. President Truman, who did not share, or did not understand, Roosevelt's policy of "accommodation" and conciliation toward the Russians in Eastern Europe, was extremely suspicious of Russia's activities there, especially in Poland. Truman was uncertain, in the beginning, whether to accommodate the Russians with concessions or to move toward a tougher stance, or, as he put it, to stop "babying the Soviets." Many of his diplomatic advisors, however, cognizant of America's unique military and economic power in the world, wanted to substitute economic power and the threat of the atomic bomb for traditional Grand Alliance diplomacy to force the Russians to hold free elections in most of Eastern Europe and to force the Russians to accept the results of those elections whether those governments were "friendly" to the Soviet Union or not. The Russians refused and Stalin's efforts to protect his nation with buffer states — or to extend his empire, depending on the point of view — prompted a major shift in American foreign policy away from "accommodation". Within weeks after the death of Roosevelt, Truman had tongue-lashed the Russian foreign minister, Molotov, abruptly cut off American lend-lease aid to Russia, and "accidently misplaced" the Soviet application for a loan. At the Potsdam conference in July, 1945, Truman and Churchill lowered the reparation figure that Russia could extract from Germany, and American officials made it clear that American economic aid to Russia would be given only after Russian behavior in Eastern Europe had improved. As Diane Clemens notes in her recent book on Yalta: "Truman set out to implement the Yalta agreements by changing them." Relations between the Soviet

Union and the United States and its allies rapidly deteriorated. In March, 1946, Sir Winston Churchill delivered his famous "Iron Curtain Speech," an address that was warmly applauded and approved by Truman. The Grand Alliance of World War II appeared shattered beyond repair and replaced by hostility, declarations of ideological war, and an arms race between the major super powers that seemed to reach into tomorrow.

Until 1947 the Truman administration, although it had already locked horns with the Russians over several issues, had devised no long-range policy toward the Soviet Union, its satellite states or Communist liberation movements throughout the world. In that year, however, it adopted the "containment" policy, the major American foreign policy measure of the Cold War. George F. Kennan, often described as the architect of the containment policy, argued that Russian foreign policy responded not to world events but rather to Marxist/Leninist paranoia and Stalin's need to justify his own totalitarian state. Kennan argued that "U.S. policy toward the Soviet Union must be that of a long-term, patient but firm and vigilant containment of Russian expansive tendencies." The Truman administration, he concluded, should never indulge in "threats or blustering or superfluous gestures" of outward "toughness," but should instead put forward its demands on the Soviets "in such a manner as to leave the way open for a compliance not too detrimental to Russian prestige." The maintenance of free world security and economic strength would eventually force the Russians to compromise, and containment would protect the Americans and her allies if applied intelligently by exerting counterpressure wherever communism attempted to break out of its containment. This policy, an essentially defensive posture, found expression in the Truman Doctrine of 1947, which promoted American military and economic aid to "support free peoples who are resisting attempted subjugation by armed minorities or by external pressure." It also gave birth to the Marshall Plan, a massive economic aid program for Western Europe to combat communism, and to a series of American alliances, the most famous and successful being NATO. The Truman administration, in brief, had revolutionized American foreign policy by launching a crusade for democracy and embarking on a program which committed the U.S. to maintaining international order. Such a policy had been unthinkable less than a decade before, but global containment, backed by massive military power, became a factor in American foreign policy, applauded and supported assertively by the American people, the American Congress, and America's allies. The tragedy was that for all the stern diplomacy and a temporary monopoly of the atomic bomb, the U.S. was unable to force the Russians out of Eastern Europe. All it did was fracture Soviet-American relations, increase Soviet suspicions of American policies and American suspicions of Soviet policies, harden Soviet-American resolve, and maintain Cold War tensions for almost three decades. As the astute Walter Lippmann observed during the height of the Cold War conflict in 1947, the Russians refused to be contained and employed every device to break out of the "iron curtain," which from their view looked like "capitalist encirclement."

The origins of the Cold War are certainly no mystery to many American scholars. Since the beginning of the Cold War there has been almost universal American agreement about the basic assumptions and goals of U.S. foreign policy. The Cold War against communism, indeed, became its own justification, and all the actions carried out in its name were explained in the stately rhetoric of American idealism. Americans were the torchbearers of liberty, "watchmen on the walls of world freedom," in John F. Kennedy's poetic phrase. The U.S. initiated the Truman Doctrine, the Marshall Plan, and NATO to impede an imminent invasion of a prostrated Europe by an aggressive Soviet Union. Although America frequently had to resort to arms in the defense of freedom, as in Korea and Vietnam, its methods and designs were both noble and disinterested. "What America has done and what America is doing now around the world," President Johnson declared in 1965, "draws from deep and flowing springs of moral duty."

This orthodox view of the Cold War, in which U.S. policy often appears virtuous, restrained, and almost passive, was formulated during the late 1940s and early 1950s, when acute international tensions rapidly deteriorated Russian-American relations. American scholars such as Herbert Feis, Norman Graebner, and particularly George F. Kennan persuasively argued that after World War II the Soviet Union tried to expand its power through military conquest and Communist revolutions in as many countries as possible, but its aggression was restricted by reluctant but vigorous counteraction from the United States which, in Kennan's famous policy statement, "contained" the Russian advance by measures of mutual assistance and collective security in Western Europe. These scholars relied heavily on the belief that the direction of postwar policies was determined by World War II itself, during which the Western democracies had been obliged to employ Russian help in defeating Nazi Germany. These events, they maintained, had left the Soviet Union militarily dominant in eastern Europe and generally occupying a position of much greater power, relative to the Western democracies, than it had enjoyed before the war. Faced with these indisputable facts, these scholars concluded that America had very little power to influence political events in what were destined to become Russian satellites, particularly since Stalin's determined efforts to expand the Soviet sphere of influence throughout western Europe had precipitated the Cold War conflict.

The revisionist or New Left American historians, notably Barton Bernstein, Gabriel Kolko and D.F. Fleming, challenge the basic assumptions of the orthodox Cold War scholars by interpreting the position of Russia after World War II as one not of offensive strength but of defensive weakness. They argue that the military disabilities of the Soviet Union, devastated by war which produced much greater losses than those of any other Western power, dictated to the Russian leaders the absolute necessity of at least a temporary policy of postwar cooperation with the Americans. The revisionists contend, however, that America's foreign policy statesmen's implacable hostility to Russian communism not only methodically stirred them to form coalitions threatening the Soviet Union with atomic destruction and organizing the Cold War as a holy crusade, but it also prevented them from comprehending the real Russian position, a proper understanding of which might have prevented the Cold War confrontation.

The most influential writer in the revisionist field and the historian who has done most to promote a revisionist interpretation of the origins of the Cold War is William Appleman Williams, to whom most of the New Left critics owe a considerable debt. Professor Williams' work, particularly *The Tragedy of American Diplomacy* (1959), which reduces all U.S. foreign policy to economic causes, not only challenges the orthodox interpretation of the Cold War but sets against it an elaborate counterinterpretation which views American foreign policy after World War II as part of a larger pattern of "globalism" reaching back into the nineteenth century.

The crisis of American diplomacy may be defined, Williams asserts, by the conflict within and between America's ideals and practice. American ideals have included a warm and generous humanitarianism, a devotion to the principle of self-determination, and a deep-rooted conviction that other people cannot really solve their own problems satisfactorily unless they imitate the American experience and the American system. Whereas the first two ideals are compatible and complementary, they are obviously contradicted by the third. And this contradiction on the level of ideas has its counterpart on the level of policy, for in practice it is the American obsession to make the world over in the American image that has dominated American policy throughout the twentieth century. The United States follows this policy and attempts to impose alien economic and political systems upon other peoples, Williams believes, because powerful American statesmen interpret America's freedom and prosperity as dependent upon an ever-expanding American system. They see, and have always seen, expansion as the principle of our institutions, and from the very beginning, therefore, the United States has been an expansionist nation preying on its weaker neighbors, whether the precivilized Indian tribes or the weaker national states and decrepit empires on its borders. This expansionism is a strangely persuasive mirror of Frederick Jackson Turner's frontier thesis; but rather than a succession of new opportunities, each American frontier was a "great evasion." It was not democracy that renewed itself in each new "West"; it was capitalism, and American foreign policy was merely the instrument of this evasive westward thrust. Once that expansion had achieved its continental fulfillment, it directed its attention to the outer world.

The vehicle for American global expansion, Williams finds, was provided by the policy of the Open Door, "a brilliant strategic stroke which led to the gradual extension of American economic and political power throughout the world." As an age witnessing the decline of the older imperialism, the Open Door substituted a new program of "imperial expansion" that "spurned territorial and administrative colonialism in favor of an empire of economics, ideology and bases." The history of the Open Door policy, and the controversies of this period in the United States have not been over strategy but merely over tactics. The debates which followed World War I and preceded World War II were essentially concerned with differences over the best means of implementing a relationship between America and the world. "To stabilize the world in a pro-American equilibrium" has been the minimum objective of the United States policy; "to institutionalize American expansion," its optimum goal. The Cold War, in Williams' view, therefore, must be interpreted as the latest phase of a continuing effort to make the world safe for American democracy and American capitalism, a phase in which the United States finds itself increasingly cast as the leader of a world-wide counterrevolution.

Williams argues that the United States cannot with any real warrant or meaning claim that it was "forced" by the Russians to follow a certain approach or policy during the 1940s because after World War II America had a "vast proportion of actual as well as potential power *vis-a-vis* the Soviet Union." The Russians, on the other hand, faced with the enormous task of rebuilding their shattered economy, interpreted "their position in the nineteen-forties as one of weakness, not offensive strength." Stalin's negotiations with Churchill in 1944, Williams believes, demonstrated that Russia had committed itself, by the end of the war, to a compromise settlement with the Americans on the need for governments in Eastern Europe not necessarily Communist but friendly to the Soviet Union, a settlement, incidentally, that required the Russians to withdraw support from the Communist revolution in Greece which, under the terms of the Churchill-Stalin agreements, had been conceded to the western sphere of influence.

American statesmen, however, according to Williams, were in no mood to compromise, for they were extremely confident of America's strength and of Russia's weakness. Armed with the atomic bomb, which intensified America's sense of omnipotence, and fortified with the beliefs, as Dean Acheson informed a Congressional committee in 1944, that "we cannot have full employment and prosperity in the United States without the foreign markets," and as President Truman put it in April, 1945, "that America should take the lead in running the world in the way that the world ought to be run," the United States government vigorously pressed for the Open Door policy throughout the world and attempted to force the Russians out of Eastern Europe. Despite the overwhelming American strength, however, the Russian leaders, who were naturally suspicious of American actions, both refused to back down and stiffened their resistance to American pressure. Not only did the Soviet Union successfully resist American demands in Eastern Europe, it launched a steady counterrevolution in the form of the Czechoslovakian coup of 1948 and the Berlin blockade. Both East and West thus found themselves fully committed to the policy of the Cold War, a conflict that is expensive and at times frighteningly dangerous.

Professor Williams' provocative and controversial analyses on the origins of the Cold War and on the failures of America's Open Door policy to change with the times make fascinating reading, for he is a facile writer and an articulate essayist. But he is obsessed by an almost exclusively economic interpretation of foreign policy that often tends to ignore material that does not support his thesis, and he dismisses rather than answers what he considers the mistaken ideas of most of his fellow historians. Williams has tended to be influenced by the sources which present primarily one side of the picture of American-Russian relations, and while the extensive documentation he provides for the American half of the story warrants careful consideration, his limited treatment of the aims and methods of Soviet foreign policy avoids the essential questions. American diplomacy, moreover, has not manifested the consistency that Williams attributes to it. It has, instead, fluctuated between the desire to project the American system upon the world at large at the partial sacrifice of self-determination, and the desire to realize the pure ideal of self-determination of an international order in which American interests might be more easily safeguarded. In judging the foreign policy of a nation, the decisive question is not whether it seeks security rather than power per se, but whether its conception of security is compatible with the security of other nations. On this important factor, Professor Williams has virtually nothing to say.

Despite these limitations, however, Williams' work on American diplomatic history has had a powerful impact upon a group of young diplomatic historians, and he has become the intellectual inspiration to a number of revisionist scholars, the most important and respected being Walter La Faber and Gar Alperovitz. Professor La Faber's latest work, *America, Russia, and the Cold War, 1945-1966* (1967), traces the relationship between the domestic and the international phases of the Cold War and the struggle between the Cold War ideology and the critical forces in the United States. He demonstrates through detailed documentation how much of the Cold War anxieties and of America's responses was due not to Russian actions but to America's interpretation of them. The rise of the Cold War, La Faber argues, was neither surprising nor remarkable; rather, the rapid decay of American-Soviet relations in 1945, visible in the uneasy wartime alliance, was rooted in preceding decades of American hostility to the Bolshevik state. Though he seems ambivalent about whether different American policies might have allayed Stalin's fears of capitalist encirclement, La Faber concludes that American ideology and actions were chiefly responsible for the Cold War. The dominant concern of American statesmen, he finds, was the need to establish an international economic system that would provide expanding markets for American surpluses and contribute to international peace and prosperity.

Gar Alperovitz's *Atomic Diplomacy: Hiroshima and Potsdam* (1965) adds very little to the interpretation formulated by Williams and other revisionist historians, but he provides their insights with a mass of additional documentation. He reconstructs the evolution of American policy between March and August, 1945, and concludes that the real reason for the use of the atomic bomb on Hiroshima was not victory over the Japanese, but intimidation of the Soviet Union in Europe. President Truman, anxious to reveal the full extent of American power to the Russians, ordered the bombing of Hiroshima in order to acquire room for political maneuvers in Eastern Europe. Alperovitz believes that this American action was done wantonly, for an unrelated purpose, in a policy that was not even directed against the enemy but against an ally. At the Potsdam Conference, the Western statesmen, armed with the awesome power of the atom, tried to pressure the Soviet Union for political concessions in Eastern Europe. The Russians, however, stood firm, and the American actions instead of achieving even partial success had, as Secretary of War Henry F.

Stimson observed, "irretrievably embittered" American-Russian relations, established mutual distrust, and created a cold war climate.

It would be an injustice to dismiss the revisionists' analyses as being little more than a confusing concoction of the "devil theory" of diplomacy and war and of a thinly disguised Marxism. Unfortunately, however, they seem almost to have gone out of their way to encourage such a judgment, for they frequently project a conspiratorial interpretation of history and cast dark allusions about the sinister influence and intentions of the various individuals among America's leadership who have influenced American policy. They have inadvertently reversed the roles of heroes and villains in the Cold War and attributed too much of what happened in the last twenty-five years to American initiatives, as though diplomacy were not an inter-action of many powers. The revisionists, indeed, suffer from what one might describe as ideological myopia: American diplomats can do no right; Russian leaders can do no wrong. The revisionists' central theme of the unhappy continuity of America's Open Door "imperial expansion," moreover, is highly debatable, as is their interpretation of the mainspring of Soviet foreign policy — a greatly relevant factor in any discussion of the American position. The revisionists have also failed to prove satisfactorily that the postwar coexistence could have been anything but antagonistic. In certain respects it might even be reasoned that the phrase "Cold War" exaggerates the gravity of the situation, for there were no war plans, no concerted effort to achieve well-defined aims, and no proof has been established that either Stalin or Truman was plotting the destruction of the other's power.

Despite these criticisms, however, the revisionist Cold War historians deserve plaudits, for revisionism is an essential part of the process by which history enlarges its perspectives and enriches its insights. Their work serves as a useful antidote to the self-congratulatory note that may be found among many of the post-World War II American historians. More importantly, however, the revisionists have clearly demonstrated that dia-metric labels such as "wicked" and "virtuous," or "aggressor" and "peace-loving nation" have little meaning in a conflict as complex as the Cold War. Much of the recent literature on the Cold War reveals that both East and West view the enemy as an outlaw against whom no holds are barred and that each side feels righteous about its cause. Louis Halle, a former member of the State Department's Policy Planning staff, in his reflective *The Cold War As History* (1968), pleads for an understanding of the Soviet Union's motives and concludes that Stalin was as much afraid of America as America was afraid of him. By carefully and critically examining the sources of the Cold War, finally, the revisionist historians have contributed to a thawing-out process, have loosened up the ideological rigidities, have greatly helped to "de-ideologize" the antagonisms of the conflict, and, most important of all, have helped to pave the way for an American policy of coexistence in international affairs to take root and to flourish.

President Truman's successors modified his global Cold War policy only in details. Presidents Eisenhower, Kennedy and Johnson, although increasingly aware of the limitations of America's power to police the world, nonetheless essentially maintained the traditional Cold War rhetoric, a rhetoric that helped to produce a series of crises in world politics during the 1950s and 1960s, the most notable being the Cuban Missile Crisis in 1962 and the Vietnam War. But with the accession to power of Richard Nixon in 1969, and with the emergence of Dr. Henry Kissinger as Nixon's chief (and eventually sole) foreign policy advisor, a changed direction in American foreign policy was institutionalized. Kissinger was a relatively obscure academician before 1969, but his rise to power and fame were extraordinary and he eventually emerged as a celebrated and powerful personality, a charismatic and glamorous figure in a position (Secretary of State) that has often been filled with mundane diplomats. For several years Kissinger's reputation and honor were above reproach. He was described as "Super K," the "Merlin of modern diplomacy," the "Secretary of the World," and "America's Metternich." His private life was reported in detail not only by infamous gossip columnists but also famous political commentators; his "shuttle diplomacy" to foreign capitals was always front-page news; his books, particularly *A World Restored* (1964), were searched and researched, assessed and reassessed, for clues to his behavior and beliefs. Kissinger's apparent foreign policy successes in Southeast Asia, which won him a Nobel Peace Prize, and his public personality, which won him world renown, propelled him so successfully into the limelight that he was viewed by the American people as the most respected man in the nation, and, in what appears to be the most anomalous observation of the past decade, the Miss Universe contestants of 1973 voted him the "greatest man in the world today." The culmination of the Kissinger mystique, the Kissinger legend, occurred in an apocryphal story that circulated during the Summit meeting in Vienna in 1973 when, after a serious negotiating meeting with Soviet leaders, an anonymous man rushed up to Dr. Kissinger, shook his hand, and thanked him for saving the world. Kissinger replied: "You're welcome."

Kissinger's achievement in promoting and creating the Kissinger mystique now appears as an almost deliberate, calculated policy on his part to create a public personality that could transcend even his own spectacular accomplishments in foreign affairs, for he exhibited none of the mercurial traits in his private academic career at Harvard that dominated his public career in Washington. Part of the answer to the Kissinger legend lay in his ability to court the press assiduously. A charming, clever and witty man, he made good copy and knew how to feed the press, massage its substantial and collective egos, and wisely separate himself from unpopular domestic issues, and, as Watergate proved, even divorce himself from a corrupt President. Part of the answer lay in Kissinger's own political talents, his ability to stand alone, his success in convincing people of his own brilliance and indispensability. Part of the answer for Kissinger's success, more importantly, is to be found in his arriving in Washington at the right time. Kissinger has surely been made by history, for the moment was ripe internally for a revolutionary change in American foreign policy. He recognized that the U.S. and the world were in a fluid, transitional period, for the nuclear superpowers were able finally to appreciate the limits of their own power and the need for reducing tensions, promoting rapproachment, and reaffirming detente. The United States, he saw, was no longer able to regard itself as the policeman of the world, for the long, frustrating years of war in Vietnam had gravely altered America's image of itself. More importantly, he understood that the strategic and military advantage the United States once enjoyed over the Soviet Union was now lost and that the traditional American Cold War policy interpretation of world communism as a monolithic creature satanically committed to the destruction of the "free world" was a misreading of history. Kissinger found American foreign policy in an almost bankrupt posture, frozen in outmoded attitudes, and he revised the prevailing American hostility to the Communist world, giving recognition to the Russian revolution of 1917 and the Chinese revolution of 1949. This acceptance, this "legitimization" of Communist regimes over these huge land masses, was a major shift in American foreign policy, for it changed the traditional United States policies of attempting to undermine these regimes by external pressure and by the "containment" of "liberation" revolutions throughout the underdeveloped Third World for the more realistic policy of "legitimacy" — the United States' exploitation of the Russian-Chinese split for the tactical and strategic advantage of the United States. Kissinger recognized what numerous scholars had recognized over a decade ago — that both the Soviet Union and the Chinese were not partners of world revolution but were, in fact, essentially status quo powers, seeking security and coexistence in an explosive age, and that they were willing to give at least partial support to American objectives in the world if they were both "legitimatized" and incorporated into the American structure of peace in which they had a stake.

Dr. Kissinger not only altered the direction of American global politics but also changed the rhetoric of the Cold War. He revised the militant and provocative Cold War slogans of the State Department and Pentagon traditionalists, who had been unable to assimilate into their ideological model of world politics the realities of global politics. In place of the John Foster Dulles missionary zeal for "wars of liberation and massive retaliation," Kissinger substituted detente and co-existence. In place of the grandiose foreign policy goals of the Eisenhower, Kennedy and Johnson administrations, he substituted the more modest goal of stability, and in so doing he rapidly and radically revolutionized American foreign policy and its official world view.

Part of the answer, finally, for Kissinger's remarkable success stemmed, of course, from his own talents and accomplishments. History played a major role in the making of Dr. Kissinger, but it is also clear that he grasped the moment to make history. He reorganized the National Security Council and provided President Nixon with a series of alternatives and options on every central foreign policy issue; he was the prime force in organizing the negotiation plans for the nuclear disarmament meetings with the Soviet Union; he was instrumental in arranging Nixon's epochal meeting with the Chinese Communists; he was invaluable in establishing the groundwork for the historic Russian rapproachment. Much of Kissinger's notable reputation as a foreign policy wonderman was richly deserved, for he was an able, intelligent and practical negotiator, untainted by any ideological premises. He always attempted to attain the attainable; he always attempted to push aside the utopian illusions that have often dominated American foreign affairs to achieve stability, balance and security. To Henry Kissinger the changed feature of international politics added up to a unique moment in history. He always considered timing as critical in any successful foreign policy venture. Opportunities, he once wrote, "can not be hoarded; once past, they are irretrievable." Not only *what* to do but *when* to do it, therefore, became one of the major features of his personal diplomatic style. Kissinger's ability to exploit the moment of opportunity to create a more relaxed, more stable, if still explosive world during the last decade was the most significant factor in establishing him as the most successful foreign policy practitioner in American history.

The Kissinger system, if it can be called that, was based upon the traditional foreign policy assumptions of the United States government, the traditional goals of peace, security, and the balance of power. The key to his foreign policy postures is through an understanding that his theories of global strategy were always predicated on the proposition that there is a necessary interrelationship among diplomacy, military strategy, ideology, the negotiations themselves, and internal domestic policies, because these factors give nations alternatives, the single most important factor in international affairs. Kissinger saw choice as fundamental to the entire political process, the prerequisite of any stable international order. Since stability is the optimum goal of an international system, the main objective of any diplomat is to devise various methods to achieve it. In Kissinger's system, international stability always depends, in Kissinger's own words, on there "being a generally accepted legitimacy," an international agreement "about the nature of workable arrangements and about the possible aims and methods of foreign policy." Kissinger developed in his writings and in his professional role as Secretary of State a distinction between two types of international order: one as "legitimate" and the other as "revolutionary." These two systems have always been apparent categories for him, and the statesman who confused one with the other, or who suffered the illusion that he was negotiating with one when he was in reality dealing with the other, was doomed to failure and would always commit diplomatic blunders. Wars can be part of the "legitimate" order, according to the Kissinger system, as long as the diplomats of the belligerent states are aware that such conflicts must be limited in goals and that the issues at stake can always be open to negotiation. Kissinger's definition of diplomacy has always been simple; "the adjustments of differences through negotiation." Nations that accept a particular international order as "legitimate" are always in a position to compromise, to negotiate their differences. Whenever a state, however, concludes that the international order is illegitimate because it circumscribes its power or discriminates against it and attempts to revise, or worse, to challenge the existing order by substituting another system in its place, then negotiations become impossible, for "revolutionary" states and "legitimate" states do not speak the same language. Whenever such a condition exists between "legitimate" and "revolutionary" states, pandemonium, chaos, instability, indeed, anarchy in international affairs reign, and the diplomats of the world become like the architects of the Tower of Babel.

Kissinger's greatest success has been as an educator, seeking to communicate his ideas, his system, his vision to other diplomats throughout the world and throughout the United States. He has always been less interested in the techniques of diplomacy than in the objectives of negotiations. In Kissinger's mind, a gifted statesman's talents are essentially intellectual and psychological: that diplomat has to know how to gauge the objectives of states different from his own; he has to judge accurately the real relationship of force to global goals; he has to possess a vision of international stability and understand how to translate that vision into a workable system; he has to be aware of history and estimate the impact of the past upon the present and future; he has to know the limits of perceptions of both friend and foe alike; he has, above all else, to comprehend and seek the possible in international affairs. In his mind Kissinger interprets a twentieth-century American statesman neither as a figure of history nor as a hero, but simply as a diplomat seeking and applying principles that can make it possible for nations in the twentieth century to avoid the terrors of nuclear war.

Although Kissinger has retired from public life, his policies are still the mainsprings of American foreign policy. These policies, detente and coexistence, stability and "legitimacy," are still being worked out, still being tried and tested, enlarged and contracted, by the Carter administration. And, ironically enough, that is still one of the major problems of American foreign policy, for though the rigid policies and rhetoric of the Cold War have dissipated, they have been replaced by a new rigidity, a new rhetoric, almost as dangerous as that of the Cold War. Kissinger himself recognized the danger, warning that

> throughout history, the primary concern of most national leaders has been to accumulate geopolitical and military power. It would have seemed inconceivable, even a generation ago, that such power once gained could not be translated directly into advantage over one's opponent. But now both we and the Soviet Union have begun to find out that each increment of power does not necessarily represent an increment of usuable political strength.

This weakness in Kissinger's balance of power system has become painfully obvious during Jewish-Arab conflicts, the Indian-Pakistan crisis, the Vietnam War, and, of course, the explosive black-white confrontations in Africa, for despite all the adjustments and counteradjustments by the major powers wars still break out. American diplomats are, unintentionally, often prisoners of the past, victims of the illusion that today is still the comfortable world of Versailles or Yalta, when a few self-appointed diplomats could make a deal for the rest of mankind. Unfortunately, we now live in an era of "monkey-wrench" politics, an age when the weak and dispossessed nations of the world, such as the Vietcong or the Palestinians, use terrorism as weapons to impose their presence upon the great powers, and until some accomodation is made for these practitioners of the politics of desperation, any attempt to establish a "Kissingerian" status quo system of peace is doomed to failure. Perhaps what is needed in the United States State

Department is a new appraisal of the objectives and methods of American foreign policy. Perhaps what is needed is a new revolution in American foreign affairs. A recognition of the Third World aspirations, an acute understanding that the best hope for American security and world peace is through a controlled disarmament and the creation of an international system in which *everyone* has a stake in the international structure of peace.

SUGGESTED READINGS

The books cited in the text by Diane Clemens, W. A. Williams, Louis Halle and Gar Alperovitz should all be consulted. Good general accounts of the origins of the Cold War can be found in John Lukacz, *A History of the Cold War* (1961), John Spanier, *American Foreign Policy Since World War II* (1971), J. L. Gaddis, *The U.S. and the Origins of the Cold War* (1972), J. V. Compton, editor, *America and the Origins of the Cold War* (1972), and G. C. Herring, Jr., *Aid to Russia, 1941-1946* (1973). The "orthodox" interpretation of the Cold War can be found in G. F. Kennan, *American Diplomacy, 1900-1950* (1951), Herbert Feis, *From Trust to Terror* (1970), Norman Graebner, *Cold War Diplomacy: American Foreign Policy, 1945-1960* (1962), Lynn Davis, *The Cold War Begins* (1974), and in the essay on the "Origins of the Cold War" by A. S. Schlesinger, Jr., in *Foreign Affairs* (1967). In addition to the books by Williams, La Faber and Alperovitz, the best "New Left" accounts of the Cold War are found in D. F. Fleming, *The Cold War and its Origins* (1961), Ronald Steel, *Pax Americana* (1967), and Gabriel Kolko's *The Politics of the Cold War* (1968) and *The Roots of American Foreign Policy* (1968). The most important and influential critique of revisionist historians is Robert Maddox's *The New Left and the Origins of the Cold War* (1973). Bernard and Marvin Kalb have written a popular biography on Kissinger (1974), but the best analysis of the Kissinger system is found in S. R. Graubard's *Kissinger: Portrait of a Mind* (1973).

CHAPTER EIGHT

The Emergence of the Imperial Presidency

DAVID D. LEE

The appearance of a strong presidency has been one of the dominant trends of twentieth century American politics. Since the succession of Theodore Roosevelt in 1901, its size, responsibility, and popular image have all changed profoundly. In the nineteenth century, the presidency was often an ineffectual institution occupied by mediocre men who took a backseat to Congress in setting federal policy. Especially during the post-Civil War years, even presidents themselves often encouraged a muted role for the office because they, like most Americans, shared the old Whig idea that the president should only execute the laws, not play any role in shaping them. As historian Leonard White put it, "The established course of the public business went on its appointed way, for the most part without requiring or inviting the collaboration of the man who sat in the White House." The twentieth century, however, saw a sharp change in this view. Campaigning for the White House in 1960, John F. Kennedy declared that on the president alone "converge all the needs and aspirations of all parts of the country, all departments of the government, all nations of the world." In short, the presidency has been remade by the events of our century into a new and vastly more powerful institution.

This strong presidency is the result of the nation's increasing obsession with complexity and crisis. The most important force in the creation of modern America was the Industrial Revolution, a nineteenth century development that completely re-shaped the socioeconomic structure of the United States by forging a specialized, interdependent economy. Prior to 1850, small farmers and businessmen were the staple of American society. Usually very individualistic, they lived in isolated areas or small towns and had few dealings outside their own communities. The Industrial Revolution changed this because it brought large industrial combinations built around mass production for a mass market. Moreover it spurred the growth of railroads and telegraph lines that bound the sprawling nation closer together.

Such far-reaching economic changes dictated shifts in the social fabric of America, and most significantly, a new emphasis on collective action. As the economy became more specialized and interdependent, it placed a premium on cooperative behavior at the expense of "rugged individualism." In addition, industrialization was a chaotic and frightening process that upset the secure worlds many Americans had known before 1850. To protect themselves in this different world and to gain some control over their lives, people began to organize themselves into unions, agricultural cooperatives, and other interest groups. Thus the Industrial Revolution gave birth to a new, group-oriented society in the United States.

The political response to these changing conditions was the Progressive movement. Progressives of both parties intended to reorganize government to cope with the consequences of the Industrial Revolution. They believed that in the future politics would become an arena for group conflict and the national government should serve as a referee and protector of the public interest. Among those who embraced this view was Theodore Roosevelt, the young New York progressive who became president when William McKinley was assassinated in 1901. Rejecting the nineteenth century concept of the presidency, TR insisted the chief executive should be, " . . . a steward of the people bound actively and affirmatively to do all he could for the people, and not to content himself with the negative merit of keeping his talents undamaged in a napkin." Barely a year after he took office, the anthracite coal strike gave Roosevelt a chance to put his beliefs into practice. In June of 1902, the United Mine Workers struck the nation's anthracite coal mines, most of which were controlled by railroads. When the owners refused to negotiate, the deadlock seemed to threaten the nation with a shortage of coal for the winter. Citing the apparent threat to the public interest as justification, Roosevelt intervened in the strike and helped secure a settlement. This action underscored the passing of the lethargic chief executives of the nineteenth century and provided a bold precedent for the president as participant in economic disputes.

If Roosevelt asserted the power of the president to act in the public interest, another president who was influenced by the ideas of Progressivism, Woodrow Wilson, worked to increase the power of the office within government. "The President is at liberty, both in law and conscience," he wrote, "to be as big a man as he can." A respected student of politics, Wilson had long felt that Congress was unable to provide overall leadership and that the president should act as a kind of prime minister who drafted bills and steered them through the House and Senate. In a significant gesture, he became the first president since John Adams to address the Congress in person. He laid out a specific program of legislation and sent his personal representatives to the Hill to solicit votes for those measures. Thus Wilson seized the initiative in the legislative process. Just as Roosevelt had developed the idea that the president had a duty to protect the public interest, now Wilson added the notion that the president should be the real leader of government.

The power of the president began to grow partly because of changes in American society but also because Congress was unable to respond to those changes. Plagued by fragmented leadership and intense partisanship, Congress was easily hamstrung by an assortment of parliamentary devices. Since it was often unable to act on national problems, the legislative branch was frequently forced to defer to a better organized executive branch. The most striking instance of this was Congress' abdication of its budget-making power. Budgeting for the federal government had usually been a Congressional responsibility vested in the Senate Finance Committee and the House Ways and Means Committee, but as the process became more complicated, these committees assigned parts of the budget to other committees. Because this left the budget to be assembled piecemeal with no central review, Congress passed the Budgeting and Accounting Act of 1921 which created the Bureau of the Budget in the Treasury Department to draw up a proposed budget. This act relieved Congress of a burdensome chore but since the budget is extremely important in establishing priorities and setting policy it also shifted power to the executive branch. Few other pieces of legislation did so much to nourish the future power of the presidency.

Although the early years of the century set the pattern for the growth of the office, it was the foreign and domestic crisis of the 1930s and 1940s that brought the real surge of presidential power. The central figure in this was Franklin D. Roosevelt. Like his distant relative Theodore Roosevelt and his mentor Woodrow Wilson, whom he had served as assistant secretary of the navy, FDR was deeply influenced by the Progressive movement. More than either of these predecessors, he played an active role in group conflict and in pushing his legislation in Congress, but Roosevelt and his New Dealers also had an important new attitude: They believed that government was capable of constructive social action as well. Typified by such programs as the Tennessee Valley Authority, the Rural Electrification Administration, and Social Security, the New Deal added a different dimension to federal power. This impulse to embark on constructive social programs was prompted by the enormity of the economic collapse the U.S. faced in the 1930s. The greatest depression in American history, it overwhelmed the efforts of private initiative and state and local government to ease its impact. The burden of meeting the crisis fell on the federal government, specifically the president. Congress showed little inclination to formulate its own program and instead waited to review the suggestions of the president. The result was the concentration of new power and responsibility in the hands of the chief executive.

Much of this new power came to rest with the president at least partly because of two other FDR contributions, one personal and the other structural. In personal terms, Roosevelt was able to project an image of great concern for ordinary people, and the public responded to him on a scale almost unprecedented among political leaders. Under Herbert Hoover, a single individual had handled all White House mail, but within weeks of the inauguration of FDR, the new president was deluged with letters, and a staff of fifty worked full-time on his correspondence. An anonymous assembly line worker in Detroit spoke for many when he told an interviewer that Roosevelt was the first president who could understand that "my boss is a son of a bitch." The president's shrewd use of radio, especially the relaxed "fireside chats," further enhanced this image of Roosevelt as a man who understood and cared about the problems of common people. The result of all this was to make the presidency the focus of government in the minds of most Americans. A popular and engaging man, Roosevelt thrust aside the austerity and remoteness of the office and used his wide personal appeal to establish himself and the presidency at the center of American politics.

Roosevelt's other significant contribution was the expansion of the executive branch, especially the establishment of the White House staff. This institutionalizing of the executive branch was dictated by the mounting work load facing the president. Prior to 1932, presidents usually did not work particularly hard. Wilson is said to have worked three or four hours a day while Calvin Coolidge averaged eleven hours of sleep. The New Deal changed all this. Most of the major New Deal legislation was written in the executive branch and charged the president, not Congress, with responsibility for fighting the depression. In 1937 Roosevelt forwarded to Congress the findings of the Brownlow Committee which he had established to review the administrative procedures of the executive branch during the hectic first term. "The President," the commission tersely reported, "needs help." It suggested the hiring of six administrative assistants "possessed of high competence, great physical vigor, and a passion for anonymity," plus the formation of an Executive Office of the President. After Congress approved a limited reorganization, Roosevelt implemented it with Executive Order 8248 in September, 1939, creating the Executive Office of the President to inform and advise him on major problems and to assist in planning future programs. In short, the reorganization gave the president the staff he needed to function as the manager of the government.

Students of the presidency are nearly unanimous in seeing Executive Order 8248 as a decisive moment in the development of the office. Luther Gulick of the Brownlow Committee called it an "epochmaking event in the history of American institutions." Arguing that the order "converts the Presidency into an instrument of twentieth century government," Professor Clinton Rossiter contended, "Its constitutional significance . . . is . . . momentous." More recently, former Eisenhower and Nixon staff member Stephen Hess has written, "It was a ringing manifesto for presidential supremacy, which had not been an accepted fact before the New Deal."

The impact of World War II only exaggerated these trends. The federal government as a whole grew enormously during the war years in terms of employees and budget and assumed such diverse responsibilities as sugar rationing and atomic research. Congress considered these problems to be administrative rather than legislative and so permitted the creation of numerous agencies to coordinate the war effort under the broad supervision of the presidency. As Richard Polenberg remarked in his study of America during World War II, ". . . the war speeded up the erosion of legislative and the growth of executive authority that had marked Roosevelt's years in office." By the time of his death in 1945, Roosevelt had profoundly altered the institution. "The Roosevelt legacy," Stephen Hess concluded, "was to expand the reach of the presidency and to change people's expectations of what government could and should do."

The growth of the presidency continued unabated during the administration of Harry S. Truman. Declaring it was "my responsibility to lead," the new president quickly proved himself a firm believer in the concept of a strong chief executive. He secured passage of a triad of measures that followed Roosevelt in institutionalizing the powers of the office. In 1947, Congress established a Commission on the Organization of the Executive Branch of Government. Chaired by Herbert Hoover, the first of its nineteen reports recommended the president be given broad authority to revamp the Executive Office according to his own discretion. The White House staff expanded from six hundred to twelve hundred and certain members, such as Clark Clifford, greatly influenced policy. The Full Employment Act of 1946 mandated that the government, implicitly under the leadership of the chief executive, assume responsibility for the prosperity of the economy and added the Council of Economic Advisors to the Executive Office to advise the President. The third measure was the National Security Act of 1947. Besides consolidating the armed forces under a new Department of Defense, the measure created the Central Intelligence Agency and the National Security Council to inform the president on defense questions.

Taken together, these three measures added to the president's obligations in foreign and domestic affairs while giving the staff support to meet them.

It was the mounting crisis overseas that led to the most dramatic demonstration of the new power that presidents exercised. On June 24, 1950, the North Korean army crossed the 38th parallel and attacked South Korea. Truman and his advisors saw the attack as a challenge to the concept of collective security and a test of American willingness to oppose Communist aggression. The next day, the United Nations Security Council called on UN members to assist South Korea and that evening Truman decided to commit American armed forces to combat. Although the Constitution gives Congress alone the power to declare war, Truman simply informed the Congressional leaders of his action two days later.

The administration explained its actions as a legitimate response to an intense crisis. The situation in Korea was urgent, its spokesmen argued, and the precedent was well-established that presidents could dispatch troops on their own initiative to secure important foreign policy goals. State Department attorneys cited eighty-seven instances where presidents had committed troops without securing prior Congressional approval. Furthermore, in the days of high-speed mechanized warfare, presidents needed such wide latitude to guarantee the nation's security. The Security Council resolution and the president's power as commander-in-chief provided ample legal support for Truman's action. Nevertheless, the president's defense had serious flaws. First of all, none of the eighty-seven cited precedents involved the United States in a major war. They were limited actions usually designed to protect the lives of American citizens. Certainly none was a conflict on the scale of the Korean War. Second, while a Security Council resolution might justify American intervention in terms of international law, it was not an adequate substitute for the Congressional approval the Constitution stipulated. As Arthur Schlesinger, Jr. said of the Korean involvement, ". . . Truman did a good deal more than pass on his sacred trust unimpaired. He dramatically and dangerously enlarged the power of future presidents to take the nation into major war."

The Eisenhower years brought something of a showdown between president and Congress on the issue of growing presidential power. In the past, the administrations of strong chief executives like Andrew Jackson and Abraham Lincoln were followed by long periods in which Congress jealously reasserted its power. The 1950s seemed to be a perfect time for such a Congressional resurgence, because the new president had a reputation as a political novice and had repeatedly stated his belief that the presidency had become too strong during the New Deal and Fair Deal. Nevertheless the Republican Eisenhower fought as tenaciously to preserve his power as any of his Democratic predecessors. An early clash came over the constitutional amendment proposed by Republican Senator John Bricker of Ohio. The Bricker Amendment was offered in several versions but essentially it provided that treaties and executive agreements would have no force in the United States without enabling legislation from Congress. To an extent, the amendment reflected the Republican charge that Roosevelt had made executive agreements detrimental to the national interest at such wartime conferences as Yalta, but basically it was an attempt by Congress to declare its authority in foreign policy. The amendment at one time claimed fifty-seven Senators as backers, but the opposition of Eisenhower and Secretary of State John Foster Dulles prevented Bricker from securing the two-thirds vote he needed.

More sinister was the challenge mounted by Senator Joseph McCarthy of Wisconsin. McCarthy had long made the executive branch a major target of his communists-in-government theme, focusing first on the State Department and later on the Defense Department. In fact, a prime ingredient of the Senator's power was his ability to exploit the traditional rivalry between the executive and legislative branches. As part of his campaign, he was eager to secure access to security files on personnel in the executive branch, specifically those held by the Department of Defense. To block McCarthy's efforts, Eisenhower proclaimed a near total presidential prerogative to withhold information from Congress. Most previous presidents had insisted that their written and oral communications were not subject to Congressional scrutiny arguing that "executive privilege" was necessary to maintain the separation of powers. Eisenhower now broadened that definition to include communications among all people in the executive branch. This new interpretation not only stymied McCarthy but also increased the power of the executive branch to deny information to Congress and made it easier for the executive branch to operate in secret, free from Congressional review.

In addition to these institutional victories, the Cold War also helped to expand presidential power during the Eisenhower years. Since the nation seemed to face the threat of armed conflict at potential flashpoints around the globe, the United States began to underwrite an elaborate system of anti-Communist alliances that spread across Asia and the Middle East. As certain areas became especially volatile, the president asked Congress to pass joint resolutions that provided him with virtual blank checks to respond as he felt necessary. In 1955, Eisenhower secured a joint resolution authorizing military action around Formosa and two years later won a similar resolution directed at the Middle East. In passing these resolutions, Congress further diminished its once exclusive war-making power while the power of the chief executive increased. Thus the ongoing confrontation with the Soviet Union broadened presidential power even with a "Whiggish Republican" like Eisenhower in office.

During his brief three-year presidency, John F. Kennedy also found in the Cold War a reason for the vigorous exercise of presidential power independent of Congressional action. The Cuban Missile Crisis represents a classic display of presidential power during intense crisis. For one of the few times in the post-war era, the United States and the world faced the distinct threat of nuclear annihilation. Operating through a small group in the executive branch, Kennedy managed the situation without any formal consultation with Congress. Unfortunately, the missile crisis has been portrayed as the rule rather than the exception in the conduct of foreign policy. Although the United States has faced a crisis of that magnitude only once in thirty years, Kennedy's action in that unique situation has been cited as justification for considerable presidential independence in the conduct of foreign policy. It was this attitude that made possible Kennedy's more questionable policy in South Vietnam. When he took office, the United States had only a few hundred military personnel in Vietnam, but Kennedy steadily increased that figure to some sixteen thousand "advisors" by the time of his death. Unlike the Korean situation, there was no overt invasion of South Vietnam nor was there a call for action by the

United Nations that could throw a cloak of legality over American involvement. Moreover the United States had no treaty obligation to South Vietnam and there were few American civilians to protect. Nevertheless, the administration took the same position the Truman administration had taken, namely that its actions were the legitimate response of the commander-in-chief to Communist aggression that threatened American security. Congress acquiesced as it had a decade earlier, even though the president had once again committed large numbers of troops to a foreign war without Congressional authorization.

Kennedy also expanded the power of the office in domestic affairs through his use of the White House staff. He was acutely aware of his responsibility as chief administrative officer and was bitterly frustrated by the unresponsive nature of the bureaucracy. Asked about his response to a certain proposal, Kennedy replied that although he favored it, he doubted the government would accept it. Part of Kennedy's solution to this problem was to widen the authority of the White House staff to make policy. As a consequence, government departments were sometimes cut out of the policy process or became subordinate to White House aides. This was especially true in foreign policy. The president considered the State Department stodgy and unimaginative, so he relied heavily on his National Security Advisor McGeorge Bundy whose staff of academics was more in tune with Kennedy's approach to the world. The State Department and Secretary of State Dean Rusk drifted out of the major policymaking process while Bundy and his intellectuals became preeminent. A similar development took place to a lesser degree in economic policy where the Council of Economic Advisors under Walter Heller became more influential with the president than the Secretaries of Commerce or the Treasury. Kennedy's approach brought a marked increase in the scope and nature of the White House staff. For the first time, it surpassed the executive departments in shaping public policy. Use of the staff enhanced the president's independence of Congress because, unlike the cabinet officers, staff members do not require Congressional confirmation and cannot be forced to testify before Congressional committees. Consequently, the president had greater freedom to shape policy without Congressional interference.

The "imperial presidency" climaxed in the 1960s and 1970s with the war in Vietnam and the Watergate cover-up. In ordering large numbers of American troops to Vietnam, Lyndon Johnson believed he was following a well-established precedent permitting the commander-in-chief to use troops to secure foreign policy goals. Roosevelt had sent the Navy to patrol the North Atlantic even before Pearl Harbor, Truman had sent troops to Korea, and Kennedy had begun the build-up in Vietnam. However, Johnson conceded the wisdom of some sort of Congressional endorsement so he secured passage of the Gulf of Tonkin Resolution which he felt authorized him to take any action necessary to advance American interests in Southeast Asia. First Johnson and later Richard Nixon considered Vietnam a "presidential" war and rarely consulted Congress on its conduct. Fittingly, when U.S. participation ended in 1973, the agreement was negotiated by a presidential aide, Henry Kissinger, rather than the State Department, and the document took the form of an executive agreement rather than a treaty that the Senate would have to approve.

The tragic involvement in Vietnam had important consequences for the presidency. The repeated blunders and miscalculations that characterized American policy seriously undermined the assumption that the presidency was inherently superior to Congress in the conduct of foreign policy. Johnson and Nixon, like earlier presidents, insisted that they alone had "all the facts" and therefore were in a special position to make important decisions, but this mistake in Vietnam greatly discredited this view. In addition it stirred a once docile Congress, especially the Senate, to challenge the president for leadership in foreign policy. Throughout the conflict, the Senate Foreign Relations Committee chaired by J. William Fulbright became a forum for antiwar spokesmen. The war was the central issue in 1968, when two other Senators, Eugene McCarthy and Robert Kennedy, challenged Johnson's renomination for president and again four years later when Senator George McGovern opposed Richard Nixon in the fall campaign. In short, the Vietnam War destroyed the myth of presidential infallibility in foreign policy and boosted the vitality of Congress.

The Watergate crisis and the disgrace of Richard Nixon further discredited the presidency. Like Johnson, Nixon began by following what he considered to be a well-established precedent. He shared John Kennedy's concern that the federal bureaucracy was unresponsive to presidential leadership and accepted Kennedy's view that the White House staff should have broader authority. Forming the core of the Nixon staff were three aides referred to collectively as the "German Shepherds." National Security Advisor Henry Kissinger was the president's ranking foreign policy expert, completely over-shadowing Secretary of State William Rogers. The domestic equivalent of Kissinger was former Seattle attorney John Ehrlichmann who took broad responsibility for social and economic policy. Perhaps most important was chief of staff H. R. Haldeman who controlled the access of both people and paper to the president. With the exception of John Mitchell, most cabinet officers were so thoroughly excluded from major decisions that one of them, Secretary of the Interior Walter Hickel, resigned, protesting he could not even see the president. The staff system gave Nixon more direct and effective control over the unwieldy executive branch, but simultaneously it isolated him from other forces in the government and left him vulnerable to its misjudgments.

Beyond this, the Nixon administration had a tendency to paranoia that gradually developed into a "bunker mentality." Believing it was under constant assault by enemies, the administration began to use the power of the government to fight back. It compiled a bizarre "enemies list" that included such people as Paul Newman and Joe Namath. Wiretaps appeared on the telephones of newspaper reporters and govern-ment officials, and John Ehrlichmann authorized the burglary of the office of a Los Angeles psychiatrist to secure information on Pentagon Papers informant Daniel Ellsberg. This trend reached a peak in the 1972 presidential campaign as officials of the Committee to Re-Elect the President pressured businessmen for contributions and played "dirty tricks" on their opponents. Most portentous of all was the ill-fated attempt to break into the Watergate headquarters of the Democratic National Com-mittee in June of that year. When the burglars were arrested, the president and several top aides tried to conceal White House involvement in the operation but Congress, the courts, and the press gradually exposed a high-level criminal conspiracy to obstruct justice. Haldemann, Ehrlichmann, and Mitchell were jailed for their participation and Richard Nixon was forced to resign in disgrace.

Like Vietnam, Watergate and the abuses of the Nixon administration greatly weakened the presidency. The damage was made worse because some of the basic institutions of the modern presidency were used in the Watergate cover-up. The White House staff had been deeply involved in Watergate-style activities and made the key decisions on the cover-up. Executive privilege and national security were invoked to keep incriminating evidence from the special prosecutor and the Senate Watergate Committee. By contrast, Congress handled the situation with great skill and added to its public prestige. The Senate Watergate Committee conducted a dignified investigation amid intense publicity while the House Judiciary Committee debated the impeachment of the president with moderation and restraint.

The events of the last ten years suggest a few things about the future of the presidency. First of all, the president will probably remain the focal point of the government. The major impulses behind the growth of the office — the appearance of a complex industrial society and the rise of America to world leadership — all remain strong forces in contemporary society. Moreover, even the revitalized Congress of the 1970s seems to be no better able to provide overall leadership than the chaotic and unorganized Congress that Woodrow Wilson described almost a century ago. Nevertheless, the Hill is likely to be extremely critical of presidents. Gerald Ford set a near-record pace for vetoes during his brief term, while Jimmy Carter has faced stiff opposition on such matters as energy and the Panama Canal.

If the substance of the office remains the same, however, the style of presidential leadership has clearly changed. For example, James Earl Carter, who introduced himself to the nation as "Jimmy," wears jeans, builds tree houses, teaches Sunday School, and attends "town meetings." Gerald Ford cooked his own breakfast. Together they have made the office warmer and more human than it was under Lyndon Johnson and Richard Nixon, but the power and responsibility of the president remain largely undiminished. In the 1976 campaign, Jimmy Carter rode to victory in part on his criticism of strong central government in Washington, but despite his election year rhetoric President Carter has the same sign on his desk that Harry Truman once had, "The buck stops here."

SUGGESTED READINGS

Especially in view of the importance of the office, the literature on the presidency is not very extensive. The only comprehensive account of the accumulation of presidential power is Arthur Schlesinger, Jr., *The Imperial Presidency* (1973). Clinton Rossiter, *The American Presidency* (1960), is a dated but thorough listing of the responsibilities presidents assume. On the exercise of presidential power, Richard Neustadt, *Presidential Power* (1964) and Theodore Sorensen, *Decision Making in the White House* (1963) offer important insights. The growth of the presidential staff has also attracted attention in recent years, especially from Patrick Anderson, *The Presidents' Men* (1969) and Stephen Hess, *Organizing the Presidency* (1967). Perhaps the best analysis of the imperial presidency at its peak is George Reedy, *The Twilight of the Presidency* (1970). Also useful are presidential biographies, especially James MacGregor Burns, *Roosevelt: The Lion and the Fox* and *Roosevelt: Soldier of Freedom* (1956-1970) and Arthur Schlesinger, Jr., *A Thousand Days* (1965).

THE AMERICAN QUEST
FOR EQUALITY
AND JUSTICE

THIS SECTION DEALS WITH the complex problem of minority rights in America. Focusing on important black leaders from Booker T. Washington to Marcus Garvey to Martin Luther King, Professor Wesley Norton describes the black quest for equality and justice in American society from the Reconstruction years of the post-Civil War period to the present period of Civil Rights' movements which found their greatest expression during the 1960s. He concludes optimistically that blacks, given their political gains, are now in a strong position to move forward in their struggle for recognition and equality. Professor Charles Bussey discusses not only the black Civil Rights struggle but also the contemporaneous movements of American women, American Indians, and American Chicanos to achieve political, social, judicial, and economic equality. Perhaps because he is surveying minority achievements over a relatively short period of time, that is, beginning in the 1960s, Professor Bussey is less optimistic than Professor Norton whose historical spectrum covers the dramatic changes of more than one hundred years, when blacks moved from slavery to full political equality. In the third essay of this section Professor Francis Thompson carefully analyzes the forces in American society which have impeded struggles of minority groups for equality and justice. Among the forces which he sees hindering the advancement of groups outside the traditional American power structure are emotionalism, xenophobia, prejudice, and ethnocentrism. He urges that Americans follow those leaders "who call forth the best of human instincts" and reject those "who appeal to the fears and anxieties in the national character." It is a difficult task to convey briefly the richness and complexities of these important topics, but the editors hope that these stimulating essays will stir the reader to explore further the civil rights' question in American history.

CHAPTER NINE

The Black Movement Towards Equality

. WESLEY NORTON

It was to be another 100 years after emancipation that laws and court decisions would bring even formal equality to blacks in the United States. The struggle for equality began among the slaves and their white friends of antislavery fame. The achievement of freedom would include developments as diverse as the Civil War, Reconstruction, the career of Booker T. Washington, the legal work of the NAACP, the social changes wrought by two world wars and one depression, numerous court decisions, and the direct action of the 1960s.

The United States government gave its final amnesty to white rebels at the close of the nineteenth century. In contrast, the limited freedom and even more limited power of the emancipated blacks had been steadily declining since the compromise between southern and northern political and economic interests in 1877.

Blacks largely lost their voting rights in the South, 1890-1910. Southern states had legalized segregation in education and were reducing the public financing of black schools relative to white schools. Public facilities became increasingly segregated by custom and law. Lynchings reached a peak of 150 each year in the last two decades of the century. In 1883, the Supreme Court voided the Civil Rights Act of 1875 and, in 1896, sanctioned segregation in the separate but equal doctrine of de facto inequality. The Court upheld literacy tests and the poll tax in decisions in 1898. De facto segregation generally prevailed in the North.

The economic position of blacks tended to deteriorate. Black businessmen, in some cases, became more dependent on less affluent blacks as they lost white clients. Labor unions discriminated against black workers who also lost ground in the urban labor market as native whites claimed the better-paying jobs and immigrants competed for those which paid less. Academic theoreticians increasingly proclaimed the racial doctrines which supported racist practices. Also Republican party leaders gradually lost interest in the black voter, especially in the South.

The blacks were by no means inactive in the face of these discouragements. Some had sought opportunity by migrating westward or northward. The black churches performed economic, educational, and social services in addition to their religious functions. Fraternal and beneficial societies were formed for mutual assistance. Denominations, with the help of whites, established colleges, several of which were to achieve the distinction of Atlanta and Fisk Universities. Philanthropists provided several million dollars for black elementary schools in the South while Booker T. Washington skillfully exploited white philanthropists to make Tuskegee Institute into a large, internationally recognized vocational school. Washington even had real, if modest, influence in the administrations of Theodore Roosevelt and Howard Taft. The turn of the century also marked the beginning of the growth of the black population in northern cities which forecast a greater role for blacks in urban and national politics.

While those years were not wholly barren, the future of the black American looked bleak indeed in 1900. He was free from slavery, but equality and the social and economic fruits of freedom were still distant dreams. Blacks were frozen into poverty in southern agriculture by the sharecropping and crop-lien systems which tended to keep them in debt and leave them without the resources to buy land. Racism was so deeply entrenched that the black and his allies would have to chip away at its structure for another half-century before they made a major breakthrough.

Blacks were to differ widely among themselves on the ideas and methods which would best serve their effort to achieve equality. Leaders were of different temperaments, came from varied backgrounds, and lived in different generations. Power rivalries and personality conflicts were as predictable among blacks as any other group. Blacks had to relate to complex changes among their own people, in public opinion, and in the degree of flexibility in the white "establishment." A black leader, therefore, might change his mind about goals and methods several times during his career.

It is well for the modern student to bear in mind, too, that every idea, every tactic, and every act of personal courage among blacks in the twentieth century had precedents among his ancestors under slavery. David Walker was not even the first advocate of black power when he urged slaves to rebel in his *Appeal* written in 1829. Nat Turner was physically militant in leading the massacre of sixty whites in 1831. Frederick Douglass escaped slavery as a youth to become an orator and influential abolitionist. He also became an accommodationist within the Republican party as did Booker T. Washington later. Martin Delaney, seventy-five years before Marcus Garvey, was one of several pioneer black nationalists with a utopian vision of the black's return to Africa. Most of all, hundreds of thousands of unknown slaves survived because they subtly and vitally shaped a system in which others held overwhelming power. Millions of their descendants have done so since.

Booker T. Washington was the key figure in the black's transition from slavery to freedom. He was the most influential black in the United States from 1890 until his death in 1915. During his career as educator, he acquired an extraordinary following among both blacks and whites. Born into slavery in 1856, a youth during Reconstruction, and graduate of Hampton Institute, he became thoroughly convinced that the key to black advance was economic. Blacks must, he felt, be trained largely through vocational education to help themselves.

Washington gained instant national prominence in 1895 when he stated his views in an address to a largely white audience at the Atlanta Exposition. He was conciliatory toward southern whites but he also tried to persuade them that the prosperity of blacks would serve their interests as well. Especially pleasing to whites, North and South, was the priority he set for economic goals over voting rights and social acceptance.

Booker T. Washington has been regarded by many as an "Uncle Tom." Historian Louis Harlan, along with others, has challenged that view. To say the least, Washington's views on vocational training are interesting in view of current emphases in education. But Washington was less accommodating behind the scenes than he seemed in public. He associated on a par socially with whites in the North and abroad. He insisted that his fellow blacks manifest racial pride and he attempted, with some success, to show them how to gain self-respect through discipline. Washington secretly lobbied in state legislatures and he secretly financed cases challenging segregation before unsympathetic courts.

By present judgments, however, Washington erred in several ways. He emphasized agriculture and the manual arts which were more appropriate to that occupation than to the mushrooming industries of the United States. If he really believed it, Washington was wrong in assuming that temporary accommodation to whites would win the full rights of blacks in a reasonable time. Through the power he had over political appointments and the flow of cash from philanthropists, Washington also neutralized those blacks who believed in more aggressive tactics. Even so, in evaluating Washington, one must take into account both his personal history as a "self-made" man and the fact that the extraordinary liabilities imposed on blacks at the turn of the century did not leave much choice in the manner of resistance.

Whatever Washington's intentions, his successes, or his failures, his power inevitably declined even before his death in 1915. Some blacks and reform-minded whites had always had reservations about some of his views and were prepared to challenge him. Foremost among the critics was W. E. B. DuBois. DuBois, born in Massachusetts, was a middle class, black intellectual with a Ph.D. from Harvard. He had been an undergraduate at Fisk University and he did postgraduate study in Berlin. Early in his career he taught at Atlanta University where he conducted significant historical and sociological studies of black life.

DuBois supported Washington during the 1890s on the idea of self-help and in the promotion of black businesses, but he broke with Washington in the early 1900s. While DuBois did not oppose vocational training, he emphasized liberal arts education especially for the "talented tenth" of the black population who would then become the teachers and leaders with the intelligence and breadth of view to propel blacks forward. Washington's policy of accommodation, DuBois insisted, yielded too much to whites. His most striking difference with Washington, however, was in his belief that blacks must constantly and openly agitate for political and civil rights.

DuBois and other blacks of his age formed the Niagra Movement in 1905 in order to further his objectives. The group consciously cultivated a militant image by conducting their meetings at historic centers of antebellum abolitionism such as Boston, Oberlin, and Harper's Ferry. The Niagra group was short-lived, and its leaders and its "radicalism" were absorbed into the National Association for the Advancement of Colored People founded in 1910.

White reformers, including Oswald Garrison Villard, grandson of the famous abolitionist, William Lloyd Garrison, took the initiative in organizing the NAACP after an especially brutal race riot in Springfield, Illinois. DuBois, placed in charge of publicity and the organization's paper, *The Crisis*, was the only black officer. The NAACP drew up a platform calling for equal educational opportunity for blacks, full voting rights, and the elimination of all forced segregation.

The NAACP drew its members from the ranks of the black elite. Even so, the organization was considered radical by most whites and some blacks who preferred the accommodationism of Booker T. Washington. NAACP lawyers won their first big case when the Supreme Court struck down the Oklahoma "grandfather clause" in 1915. Since then this organization has been the leading instrument in lobbying and in maintaining pressure in the courts on behalf of black rights.

In the meantime, the urbanization of the blacks was accelerating, a factor destined to be very important in the civil rights movement. In 1910, about three of four blacks were rural and nine of ten lived in the South. During World War I, many blacks migrated to northern cities largely to improve themselves economically. This trend has continued to the present with a great acceleration of the process again during World War II. Today, about fifty percent of blacks in the United States live outside the South and the ratio of rural to urban blacks has exactly reversed itself. The black population is even further concentrated into the interior of America's largest cities.

Race riots of major proportions followed the World War I migration and were a part of the emotionalism of the Great Red Scare, 1919-1920. Blacks were still largely the victims in these riots, but they were now more inclined to aggressively defend themselves. In fact, some of the riots began when blacks resisted abuse, as in Houston in 1917 and in Chicago, Illinois and Elaine, Arkansas in 1919. Whites then retaliated with violence on a much larger scale.

In the aftermath of the riots, the rising racial consciousness of black city dwellers and their increasing sensitivity to violations of their rights led to more forceful protests. Negro soldiers who had recently performed heroically in a war to make the world safe for democracy, were likely to seek a larger share in American life. Individual acts of resistance to threats became more common and these acts found encouragement and support in the NAACP. Dr. Ossion Sweet and members of his family fired into a white mob which was attacking his home in a white neighborhood in Detroit. Having killed one of the attackers, they were tried for murder, but NAACP lawyers won an acquittal.

During the twenties, the NAACP had only limited success in the courts against segregation and restrictions on voting rights. Out of frustration came charges from the left that the NAACP was too conservative, a charge its leaders had once made against Booker T. Washington. A. Philip Randolph, editor of the radical *Messenger*, attacked the NAACP leaders including DuBois, whom he saw as the equivalent of an "Uncle Tom." He accused the middle class members of the NAACP of being indifferent toward the Negro masses. Randolph believed that capitalism was the root of social evil, therefore, black and white workers must act together against the capitalists in order to achieve their rights. Over opposition even from some fellow blacks, Randolph organized the Brotherhood of Sleeping Porters and Maids as one result of a move to unionize black workers. Most black leaders tended to mistrust unions because they practiced discrimination and, in fact, blacks were often quite willing to serve as strikebreakers.

Marcus Garvey was another voice arising among the black masses during the twenties. Garvey was born in Jamaica where he organized the Universal Negro Improvement Association in

1914. He came to New York and organized a chapter in 1916 which held a strong appeal for the masses in their ghetto squalor. Not simply problack, Garvey was antiwhite. His stated purpose was to separate blacks from whites by way of the mass migration of American blacks to Africa.

Garvey's appeals to racial pride took the form of black businesses, the African Legion, Black Cross nurses, belief in a black Christ, and parades through ghetto streets. He fell victim to charges of fraud in connection with his Black Star Steamship Company. These charges were first called to the attention of federal authorities by hostile black leaders who were among Garvey's bitterest critics. Garvey in turn had contempt for such leaders as DuBois, contending that he sought racial "amalgamation."

There were other important developments among urban blacks in the twenties. Their concentration in the cities brought them back into national politics as officeholders when Chicago blacks elected a representative to Congress in 1925. The ghetto also made possible a growing professional and business elite whose clients were drawn from the black masses. The concentration of blacks in New York resulted in the Harlem Renaissance. The "New Negro" intellectuals were militantly proud of their past and celebrated it in art and literature. The systematic study of that past had already been assured by the founding of the Association for the Study of Negro Life and History and the organization's *Journal of Negro History* commenced in 1916. The works of black writers called attention to the black experience as rich in culture both in itself and as a part of the total American heritage.

The blacks, along with many whites, did not share in the prosperity of the twenties and the Great Depression, therefore, intensified already serious problems. Blacks especially became candidates for relief, and by October, 1933, from twenty-five to fifty percent of their number in the cities were receiving public assistance. President Franklin D. Roosevelt, guided by several prominent New Dealers and his wife, Eleanor, found not only humanitarian challenge but political opportunity in the plight of the blacks.

The black voter began a gradual shift from the Republicans to the Democrats in 1924, a shift which became dramatic in the 1930s, though it lacked the totality of recent elections. Blacks were attracted to the Roosevelt style and felt directly the benefits of New Deal relief and recovery programs. They also appreciated the attentions of Mrs. Roosevelt who dramatically protested when the Daughters of the American Revolution refused Marian Anderson the use of Constitution Hall for a concert. The Lincoln Memorial then became the site for the concert, drawing to itself an impressive symbolism.

Roosevelt maintained contact with a broad collection of black advisors who worked in various government departments. This group served as an unofficial "Black Cabinet." These men used their positions to press for political equality and greater employment opportunities for blacks. The most significant gain was in the federal government itself where 200,000 blacks were employed by 1946 in contrast to 50,000 in 1933. More blacks received appointments and at higher levels than ever before in the twentieth century.

The net gain for blacks under the New Deal was very important, but the record was uneven. There were inequities in the administration of relief and in the payments to farmers under the Agricultural Adjustment Administration. While housing programs benefited many blacks, there was still segregated housing even in northern cities. The Civilian Conservation Corps included 200,000 black youths, but they were segregated throughout the system. There was no large breakthrough in bias among labor unions until the Committee on Industrial Organization gained strength in the late 1930s and early 1940s.

World War II increased the momentum of civil rights activities. Blacks found a stake for themselves once more in an international conflict which focused upon freedom from the effects of fascist dictatorial and racist practices. Also the promise of employment in war industries drew vastly larger numbers of blacks into the cities. Strong and sophisticated pressures from blacks upon New Dealers reduced the effects of segregation in the armed forces by the end of the war. When Randolph threatened to lead a massive protest march on Washington, President Roosevelt appointed the Fair Employment Practices Commission to increase the opportunities for the employment of blacks in government and in war industries. The near-full employment in the wartime economy, however, was probably the most important factor in employment gains. The actions of the FEPC did prove that the federal government could have a marked effect on employment practices.

After the war, President Harry Truman appealed successfully to the black electorate in his surprise victory in 1948. He had favored the strong civil rights plank in the Democratic platform which drove the Dixiecrats out of the party. Henceforth, the issue of equal rights was to be before the public in every national election. Under Truman, but with some balking in Congress, formal segregation finally came to an end in all branches of the Armed Forces of the United States.

By the 1950s, the climate was more favorable to civil rights as public opinion had gradually become more receptive. New expectations had risen among blacks themselves as a result of their participation in the war on the battlefield and at home. States in the North and West took more certain steps toward assuring fairness in housing, jobs, and public accommodations. The issues of the Cold War also stirred blacks in America as the United States and the Soviet Union vied for advantage among the underdeveloped nations, many of them black, which were throwing off colonialism.

The NAACP had continued to work aggressively in the courts and in the legislatures. Their lawyers had won against the white primary system of the southern Democrats in 1944. They had also pressed the attack against discrimination in education, at first challenging the less sensitive areas in professional and graduate schools. Their most significant victory came in *Brown v. the Board of Education* in 1954 when the Supreme Court ruled that separate education was inherently unequal. The equal rights "revolution" was now well under way.

As the struggle accelerated, blacks themselves took more initiative and the movement extended beyond the middle class into the masses. As the movement expanded, it naturally acquired more diversity, the most dramatic development being in the effective use of direct action techniques in the fifties and sixties. Direct action was not new, but activists used the tactics on a much larger scale and in an environment which produced more results. The demonstrators persisted in the face of violence while the violence itself shocked the rest of the nation. Even the NAACP and other older groups supported direct action largely through money, defense lawyers, and political pressure.

The newer organizations sent in the shock troops and fell in behind those individuals who directly challenged the many forms of segregation. The bus boycott in Montgomery, Alabama, in 1955-1956 was a success for economic pressure. At the same time, it brought Martin Luther King to national prominence as a civil rights leader. King professed to believe in the power of nonviolence and unmerited suffering to convert the white oppressor. In 1957 he organized the Southern Christian Leadership Conference, in name and in fact, appealing to the potentially very significant religious conscience of the American people.

The Congress of Racial Equality, formed in 1942 and led by James Farmer beginning in 1961, was the earliest of the direct action groups, and also relied on nonviolence. CORE quickly backed the sit-ins at lunch counters which were launched by students on their own initiative at Greensboro, North Carolina in 1960. CORE also sent "freedom riders" into the South to test the application of laws prohibiting segregation in interstate transportation in the spring of 1961. Southern whites intensified their resistance through the use of local police power and through their own version of direct action which, in one instance, took the form of burning buses.

The Democratic party, under the Kennedys, continued to bid for the black vote. During the campaign in 1960, candidate John F. Kennedy not only promised action on equal rights, but he and his brother Robert intervened directly to gain King's release from jail. President Kennedy appointed blacks to high office but, to satisfy his southern white constituents, he balanced those assignments by appointing segregationist judges to lower courts in the South.

In the meantime, a more radical mood developed and more radical organizations gained attention, especially among the young. Inevitably the black organizations became rivals with each other for attention, money, and power. The Student Nonviolent Coordinating Committee, founded by King in 1960, broke from him the following year. The Black Muslims experienced a resurgence, benefiting from both the recession of the early 1950s and the success of civil rights agitation. The Muslims were black nationalists reminiscent of Marcus Garvey who appealed largely to the very poor. Their leaders denounced white devils and consigned them to doom once the blacks, in a separate order, became ascendant. The radical vocabulary of the Muslims made other organizations seem more moderate and even welcome. Muslims uniquely insisted upon a rigorous moral discipline and Puritan work ethic for their members. They split into factions with violence eventually erupting among them, resulting in the assassination of Malcolm X.

The year 1963 was the centennial of the Emancipation Proclamation. Leaders consciously sought to make 1963 a turning point in the achievement of equality and they were largely successful. Demonstrators applied pressure all across the South. King articulated the American dream for blacks at the Lincoln Memorial as the climax of the march on Washington. The media effectively displayed the official use of dogs, nightsticks, and water hoses in Birmingham. A hidden assassin murdered Medgar Evers in the driveway of his home and, in September, four children died in the bombing of a Birmingham church while Sunday school was in session.

President Kennedy used the occasion of the violence to go on national television with an appeal for the passage of the new Civil Rights Bill. The bill dealt with public accommodations, voting rights, and fair employment. President Kennedy himself was assassinated in Dallas in November.

The emotions released by the assassination, strong lobbying by black groups, an indignant public, and the political skill of President Lyndon B. Johnson brought passage of the Civil Rights Act in June of 1964. For the first time, the Senate had voted cloture to break the filibuster of a civil rights measure. In 1965, the Congress passed, with Johnson's urging, the Voting Rights Act which provided for direct federal intervention in voter registration. By the end of that year, 250,000 new voters were registered in the South, one-third by federal registrars and two-thirds by local officials who yielded to the law. There have been 3,000,000 southern black voters registered since 1965.

President Johnson, wily and tainted politician though he was, had spoken movingly in behalf of equality at Gettysburg in 1963 while still vice-president. In the television speech launching his campaign for the Voting Rights Bill, he concluded with one of the key phrases of the black's cause, "We shall overcome." Just as the power and the skill of the politician, Abraham Lincoln, and his skilled and dedicated general, Ulysses S. Grant, made emancipation a fact, so Johnson's use of political power put the final cap on civil rights insofar as law can achieve them.

Although school segregation had been declared illegal in 1954, only in the 1960s was real integration accomplished in southern elementary and secondary schools. By 1968, ninety percent of public school systems were technically classified as integrated. Attention now has shifted to the de facto segregation in northern cities where the issue is still being resolved.

Martin Luther King was killed from ambush in 1968. The assassination produced riots in cities across the nation and immediately strengthened the position of the radicals. The NAACP, in spite of its consistent and varied programs, was too tame to suit the young. The "black power" of Stokely Carmichael, chairman of SNCC, was in vogue. Each organization, of course, attracted those whose temper was most suited to its methods at the time. The Black Panthers gained national attention, especially among law enforcement agencies. Blacks identified themselves with what their fancy conceived of as ancestral African homes, names, and hair styles. Race baiting was common as the liberal white became "honkey" and the less than radical black an "Uncle Tom."

Political power was the more lasting achievement, the "arithmetic of the ballot." One hundred black mayors of American cities have been elected since 1965 and two of those cities are among America's largest, Los Angeles and Detroit. The total of all elected officials has risen to 3,000 from 600 in 1965. There are sixteen blacks in Congress. The current United States ambassador to the United Nations is black. In addition, hundreds of white elected officials have heard the message of the ballot.

The United States rarely, if ever, produces lifelong revolutionaries. Those who have the intelligence, energy, talent, and will to lead are enticed into the middle class value system by their very success. Equally important, the American political, social, and economic system is eventually remarkably responsive to aggressive minorities. Some fists unclench, iced souls thaw by conversion, and panthers return to face charges with new confidence in the court of law. The economy slowly yields its fruits which most would rather have than to suffer the painful effects of violent revolution.

Even with some goals reached and others attainable,

frustrations never cease to exist for real people in a real world. The time of "revolutionary" activism is heady with youth, commitment, and romance. The actual achievement of the results of political, social, and economic equality is mundane. Furthermore, the irony of freedom is that self-realization and the fulfillment of the dream are only possibilities for the individual even after a society provides its imperfect guarantee of equality. Blacks now seem destined to strengthen that guarantee and to fulfill its promise judging by the initiative, intensity, and persistence with which they have pursued their freedom.

SUGGESTED READINGS

The textbook of black history is John Hope Franklin's *From Slavery to Freedom* . . . (1974). This book also includes a bibliography which is one of the most useful available for the beginning student. For the more serious scholar the best bibliographical aid is James M. McPherson and others, *Blacks in America: Bibliographical Essays* (1971). John Roche, *The Quest for the Dream* . . . (1968) deals with civil liberties in general in the twentieth century. Alan F. Westin, ed., *Freedom Now! The Civil Rights Struggle in America* (1964) gives the statements of many of the leaders during the climax of the civil rights movement in the 1960s. August Meier and Elliott Rudwick, *From Plantation to Ghetto* (1970) is a concise summary and interpretation of the black's movement toward freedom.

Instruction at Home; Transylvania, Louisiana, 1939. (Library of Congress)

CHAPTER TEN

Struggling American Minorities

CHARLES BUSSEY

Although the American dream defies neat packaging and defining, the means by which each group within American society is allowed to define it (the American dream) are similar. This essay focuses on the means by which four different groups have sought to define their dream, the way they have pursued it, and the status of their individual movements in late 1977.

Common to each of these groups is the theme of oppression and thus the denial of the right to define the dream in individual terms. A dictionary definition of oppression is "unjust or cruel exercise of power . . . by the imposition of burdens." A recent description of oppression is more vivid. JoAnn Ashley ("Health Care, American Style: Helter Skelter, *Par Excellence*," *Supervisor Nurse*, Feb., 1977) wrote:

> As an oppressed group in . . . life, nursing fits very aptly into the category of those coping with a culture of poverty, assuming the role of beggars and living in constant fear of not surviving. To date, we have not been fully recognized as a group having much to offer society. . . . As a result, society has not supported us and we have, in many respects remained poor. . . . We have been crippled and handicapped by poverty in spirit and in purse.

The means of breaking that authority which oppresses is through the acquisition and use of political and economic power. But without a vision of the spirit, or the acquisition of power, visibility of the group and the use of power will ultimately fail.

A young president, John F. Kennedy, challenged Americans with his campaign and inaugural rhetoric in 1960-61. His commitment to substantive reform can be questioned, but the fact that he stirred the winds of change with a call to action was real. During the first years of the Kennedy administration, critics of the American scene began to make themselves heard. Poverty, thought by many Americans to have been abolished, was rediscovered by Michael Harrington in his 1963 book *The Other America*. Harrington and other social critics pointed out the festering pockets of misery and poverty in the United States, especially among blacks, women, Indians, and Chicanos.

BLACK LIBERATION

These groups obviously did not need to be told that they were denied full sharing in the American dream, but suddenly in the early 1960s their plight became visible to the rest of the nation. The grandfather of American reform movements prominent between 1960 and 1970 was the civil rights movement for blacks, and it provided a model for those movements which followed.

Indeed, civil rights activism in the South sparked a thaw in the frozen social justice movement in the United States. Stimulated and encouraged by the Supreme Court's 1954 *Brown* v. *Board of Education* decision, which declared school segregation on the basis of race unconstitutional, demands by black Americans for civil rights moved into the forefront of American life. The movement picked up steam in 1955-56 with the emergence of a charismatic black preacher/leader, Martin Luther King, Jr., a Boston University Ph.D. as well as ordained Baptist minister. King planned and saw to execution a successful bus boycott in Montgomery, Alabama. In the end, under economic pressure from the boycott as well as legal pressure from the courts, city officials were forced to back down and desegregate their public bus system.

Following the success in Montgomery, King and other concerned Christian leaders organized the Southern Christian Leadership Conference, and shortly thereafter James Farmer and Floyd McKissick reactivated the Congress of Racial

Equality, which had been moribund since the 1940s. Another civil rights organization, the Student Nonviolent Coordinating Committee, was formed in April, 1960. SNCC evolved out of North Carolina student demonstrations in early 1960, the "sit-ins", which forced desegregation of lunch counters in that state. These new groups proved to be much more activist in orientation than the older and more sedate National Association for the Advancement of Colored People.

The Kennedy administration, which had received important aid from the black community in the 1960 election, was extremely cautious and lost the initiative to young CORE and SNCC activists in the South in 1961. Those two groups sponsored the "freedom rides" of that year in their nonviolent efforts to integrate buses and bus terminals, but the violent white response to their action forced Attorney General Robert F. Kennedy (the President's brother) to act. He ordered an FBI investigation, sent federal marshalls into the South to protect the freedom riders, and generally put the weight of the administration behind the activists. Following a Kennedy directive, the Interstate Commerce Commission entered the picture. By utilizing federal power first suggested in the 1824 *Gibbons* v. *Ogden* decision, in which the John Marshall Court held that people are commerce, the ICC outlawed segregation on/in interstate facilities.

Gradually President Kennedy's hand was being forced — blacks were calling in their election IOUs. In 1962 James Meredith determined to integrate a key link in the chain of white supremacy, the University of Mississippi in Oxford. After some hesitation, and inconclusive negotiations with Mississippi Governor Ross Barnett, Kennedy faced up to the mounting crisis and sent in federal marshalls along with several thousand federalized national guardsmen to protect Meredith. Ole Miss integrated. Two men were killed and a number injured, but the barrier had fallen, and the following year (despite Governor George Wallace's bluster) the University of Alabama fell to the integrationists without casualty.

By the spring of 1963, as action shifted from the campus to the streets, the civil rights movement gained momentum. The focal point of action that spring was Birmingham, Alabama, as concerned persons took to marches to protest the segregation of public facilities. Birmingham police chief Eugene "Bull" Connor turned on the marchers with fire hoses and dogs, a terrible moment in American history which was captured by photographers and television cameras with pictures which shocked the nation's conscience and sensibility. With the rising tide of violence used against the civil rights advocates, there were growing tensions within the movement and some disillusionment with King's nonviolent approach.

Despite the growing divisiveness among blacks over means, the greatest display of unity in this phase of the movement took place in August, 1963, three months before President Kennedy was shot and killed in Dallas, Texas. Dissension was submerged for the moment, and various groups (SNCC, NAACP, CORE, the Urban League, white and black church leaders, and labor leaders) converged to lead a march on Washington which mobilized 200,000 demonstrators. That was the setting for Martin Luther King's stirring speech, "I Have A Dream," which attempted to define the black dream, in general terms of freedom from oppression.

Freedom Summer 1964, designed by civil rights activists as a time to go into the South and register blacks to vote, witnessed the death of several of those workers and saw the intensification of tensions within the movement itself. There was more questioning of King's nonviolent approach and a decided reaction on the part of blacks against paternalistic white leadership. The movement became more violent in the summer of 1965 as Watts, a Los Angeles ghetto, exploded. Violence in America's cities reached a peak in 1967 with disorders in 128 cities and major clashes in Newark and Detroit.

King was gradually losing his grip on his people, and the term "Black Power" came into common usage. Malcolm X (formerly Malcolm Little), a black leader who rejected white leadership in any form, was killed in 1965 after breaking with Elijah Muhammed, leader of the Black Muslims, a black nationalist group. Three Black Muslims were subsequently convicted of Malcolm's murder. Perhaps more important in this phase of the action (certainly the most militant) was the development of the Black Panthers, led by Eldridge Cleaver, Huey Newton, and Bobby Seale. Cleaver had written a searing indictment of America, *Soul on Ice*, while in prison on a rape charge, and he was the most articulate of the Panther spokesmen. This element frightened Americans, even liberals, with its paramilitary garb, its naive Marxist rhetoric, and its demands for retribution from a white society which had enslaved blacks.

Not only were whites frightened by the new, more radical, definition of the American dream by blacks, but the fact that the action had moved north created a backlash. White northerners who had heretofore either supported the civil rights movement in the South, or at least remained silent, found their voices; for it was their social structure/school system/neighborhoods now being attacked as racist and segregated. They found out what should have been obvious from history: it is much easier to support oppressed people when they are thousands of miles away than when they are next door.

As passions mounted, so did violence. Martin Luther King, Jr., was killed in Memphis, Tennessee; Robert F. Kennedy, a hero to many blacks and in the midst of a presidential bid, was killed in Los Angeles; Eldridge Cleaver fled the country; the SCLC Poor People's March bogged down in the spring rains of Washington, D.C.; the movement, once so glorious, was breaking up.

The question for this essay is: What had been gained? True, many civil rights acts were passed making it possible for blacks to vote and hold office; there are currently something over 3,000 black political office holders in forty-one of the fifty states; blacks are visible in terms of television programs and commercials; but in terms of the basic economic situation, the grim reality has resulted in actual loss. Although the gap between black/white income narrowed in the late 1960s, that trend reversed in the early 1970s, and today the gap is wider. Unemployment for blacks is at least twice that for whites; and in many urban areas in the summer of 1977 black unemployment frequently ran as high as sixty percent. Presently the black community appears to lack dynamic and unifying leadership. The nearest thing to a national leader is Chicago-based Reverend Jesse Jackson, but he has yet to demonstrate the power needed to bring the liberation movement together again.

INDIAN LIBERATION

Up to 1933 whites had pursued three major policies with regard to Indians: (1) forced removal to a reservation;

(2) genocide; (3) allocation of a specific amount of land if he would renounce his culture and adopt the trappings of white society. But 1933 represented something of a turning point. Franklin Roosevelt's Commissioner of Indian Affairs, John Collier, was sympathetic to the Indian's plight and was determined "to promote a sense of pride among the Indians" by emphasizing their history, language, and customs. He was determined to do this through an infusion of federal funds to stimulate the Indian educational system. He faced stiff opposition, however, especially among Indians whose Indian-ness had been "diluted by years of pressure and proselytizing by Christian sectarian groups. . . . " Collier fought to overcome that opposition, but he was interrupted by World War II. During the war's last years, as he continued his policy of emphasizing the Indian's past and at the same time educating various tribes to the potential usage of their lands, he ran into bitter opposition from white ranchers and farmers who were in the habit of leasing Indian land at a fraction of its value.

Indians returned from World War II — 125,000 Indians participated in either a civilian or military capacity — to a dismal and isolated experience. (If you want to understand and feel that postwar trauma, listen to Johnny Cash describe the treatment accorded a World War II Indian hero in "The Ballad of Ira Hayes.") From the end of the war to the 1960s, the United States government vacillated in its treatment of the American Indian. At first the government reverted to its pre-1933 policy of trying to anglicize the Indian in terms of culture. This regressive policy continued until President Dwight D. Eisenhower's second Secretary of the Interior Fred A. Seaton, stopped it. Seaton argued that it was absurd "to force such a . . . policy upon Indians who neither comprehended nor accepted it."

In the 1960 presidential campaign between John F. Kennedy and Richard M. Nixon, both candidates advocated an Indian policy based on "self-determination programs similar to those of Commissioner Collier in the 1930s." After that the Indian problem continued to languish. In 1961 only sixty Indians in the whole country graduated from college, and the future looked bleak, and as late as 1971 fifty percent of all Indians left high school before completion. Indian life expectancy remained six years below the national average in the

1970s; and their average annual per capita income remained seventy-five percent below the national average, about a $1000 less than the average black income. The unemployment rate for Indians runs at least forty percent in the cities and as high as eighty percent on the reservation. There are about 800,000 Indians in America today and they "remain the poorest of the poor."

The American Indian's tardiness in pursuing active dissent from official government policy can be explained. His strength had been sapped after decades of almost total oppression, and he had to learn "to abandon the white man's road." For even under the progressiveness of the Collier program, "tribal councils [had been] controlled by Indians willing to take the advice of the white man." The 1960s, however, represented a new era of social consciousness and heightened interest in ethnicity. The American Indian, for so long repressed, was stimulated by the black movement to begin his demand for the right to define the American dream. Between 1961 and 1971, things began to change. In the former year only twelve Indian students could be found willing to write an Indian manifesto; in 1971 hundreds of Indians moved in and took over the Offices of the Bureau of Indian Affairs in Washington, D.C. During that decade the Indian had been radicalized.

Mel Thom, a civil engineer, was the first president of the newly established National American Indian Youth Council, and he called for activism. Accordingly, on 20 November 1969, a group of Indians took over Alcatraz Island off the California coast. Formerly a federal prison, the Indians demanded (under an old treaty which awarded unused federal land to Indians) that the twelve-acre site be made an Indian shrine and that Thunderbird University be established there. Those militants were finally removed without injury on 11 June 1971, but the Indian received a great deal of publicity and became more visible.

Encouraged, Indian protest turned more and more to activism with the organization of the American Indian Movement, under the direction of radicals Dennis J. Banks and Russell Means. Early in February 1973, A.I.M. led a rampage against whites in Custer, South Dakota, before moving on later that month to Wounded Knee, South Dakota, a trading post with little material value, but a spot with great symbolic meaning for the American Indian; for it was the site of the last great slaughter of the red man by the white. Though A.I.M. activists who occupied Wounded Knee were ultimately frustrated by federal marshalls, the taking of it was a defiant statement to the white establishment that the Indian would pursue the American dream in his own manner. The militants who led the Wounded Knee assault had a positive effect in promoting "a new pride in Indian culture, a fresh concern with preserving an ancient heritage, and a stronger determination to make whites live up to past promises."

WOMEN'S LIBERATION

An interesting element (creation) of the 1960s social justice movement in the United States was the women's liberation movement. Women have had a long history of protest in America, and their demand to be included in the American dream dates back at least to Abigal Adams' demands to be included in the new power structure in letters to her husband John while he attended the Second Continental Congress in 1776. Periodically the movement has risen to the noticeable level, especially during the reform-oriented period just before the Civil War.

Women, while achieving much visibility in the work force during World War II, faded from sight during the postwar period. But in 1963 two important events occurred which marked turning points in the struggle by women to secure the American dream. First, a Kennedy-appointed commission on the Status of Women reported that indeed women were being oppressed in terms of jobs, pay, and benefits. This rather conservative report at least recognized oppression's existence, and called for an end to discrimination within the structure of the federal government, in addition to requesting day-care centers and job counseling for women. In response the Congress that year did pass an Equal Pay Act for federal workers. But more important 1963 was the year in which Betty Friedan's compelling book *The Feminine Mystique* was first published.

Friedan's work contended that women had retrogressed since World War II and that women had been conditioned "to believe that fulfillment for any normal woman meant a life limited to home, husband, and family." This analysis was especially attractive to that middle class element where women were generally well educated and felt stultified in the kitchen. Friedan's group organized the National Organization of Women in 1966, and she was elected its first president. That organization, later called by some more radical women the NAACP of the women's movement, was mainstream, liberal, and college educated. Their basic goals were to end job discrimination, liberalize abortion and birth control laws, and provide day-care centers.

A dichotomy began to make itself felt as not all women were satisfied by that basic liberal approach. Women, many of them students, were active in the antiwar movement that accelerated in the mid-1960s. Originally they were satisfied to play a subordinate role to their male counterparts. Men organized rallies, plotted strategy, and led; women made coffee, rolled bandages, and were available sexual partners. But then, perhaps inspired by the Friedan group's rhetoric, though applying it to different circumstances, "the women's liberation movement began to challenge this situation dramatically." According to historian Irwin Unger: "Given the new sensibility of the 1960s, women's liberation was probably inevitable."

Radical women like Shulamith Firestone and Robin Morgan "denounced radical men as chauvinists" and "insisted that only women could liberate themselves." Women had to discover (like their 1840s and 1850s sisters) that working for the civil rights of others, or against an unjust war, would not assure them their own rights.

In 1967 Jo Freeman in Chicago "organized the first women's consciousness-raising group" in America, and two years later a group of radical women issued a manifesto:

> Women are an oppressed class. Our oppression is total, affecting every facet of our lives. We are exploited as sex objects, breeders, domestic servants, and cheap labor. We are considered inferior beings, whose only purpose is to enhance men's lives. Our humanity is denied.

Just as NOW's earlier rhetoric had originally encouraged antiwar/civil rights activists, the more radicalized women liberationist statements such as the one quoted above strongly influenced NOW, as it moved much further in its demands to be included in the American dream.

As America moved into the mid-1970s, the women's

liberation forces appeared to be coming unglued. For example, the Equal Rights Amendment to the United States Constitution, six years into the ratifying process, is stymied. Thirty-five of the necessary thirty-eight states have ratified; but there seems to be no steam left in the movement to push it over. The deadline for this amendment is March 1979, at which time it will die if not ratified. An issue which has proved especially divisive among women is the question of abortion. That this is so is evidenced by the intense pro/con reaction to the recent decision by President Jimmy Carter and HEW Secretary Joseph Califano (and legitimized by the Supreme Court) to deny the use of federal funds for abortions except for cases involving special circumstances such as pregnancy by rape or the threat of death to the mother if the pregnancy is allowed to go to term. The two major problems facing the women's movement today are the failure to bring the poor into the movement and the failure of a charismatic leader similar to King or Chavez to instill at least some sense of unity among women. If the poor can be involved in the movement (the abortion decision reflects their lack of power), and if a new leader emerges (Gloria Steinem will not do), this movement may advance with renewed vigor.

CHICANO LIBERATION

While the hostility and racism which the Chicano faces today is not new, his reaction to oppression is clearly a product of the American scene in the 1960s. In fact, the term Chicano did not come into existence until 1968 when young radicals rejected the older term (Mexican American) as too conservative, as an effort to destroy the Mexican's association with his past.

Large-scale discrimination practiced by the Anglo against the Mexican American had started when Washington politicos manufactured a war in 1846 in order to acquire vast stretches of Mexican territory, including California. The Treaty of Guadelupe Hidalgo, which ended that war, contained clauses which guaranteed Mexicans (living on what had just become American soil) first-class citizenry with protected life, liberty and property. Those guarantees, however, were ignored and in the words of historian Rodolfo Acuna "the Mexican became a second-class citizen in what was formerly his land."

Not only was the Mexican's right to live his own life-style denied, but he was subject to indiscriminate violence and was openly terrorized. Walter Prescott Webb, famous Texas historian, has estimated that in a great wave of terror in 1915 the Texas Rangers killed between 500 and 5,000 Mexicans in an "orgy of bloodshed." Moving through the twentieth century, the Mexican American continued to suffer at the hands of the Anglo establishment, though not always to the same bloody extent.

During the Great Depression of the 1930s, for example, hundreds of thousands of Mexicans were repatriated from the American Southwest in order to ease the unemployment situation in the United States. While there was some protest, which continued on a small scale during and after World War II, such remonstrance had little success — it was essentially invisible. The 1952 McCarran-Walter Act of the United States Congress allowed the denaturalization of any naturalized citizen who had ever belonged to a subversive organization. The fact that the Attorney General's Office so defined subversive organization as to include various relief agencies as well as labor unions was effectively used to get rid of any Mexican activists who might "cause trouble." The McCarran-Walter Act plus the widespread use of braceros (contract workers brought into the United States from Mexico) by agribusiness undercut any effort by Mexicans to define or realize the American dream.

As the American nation moved into the 1960s a new age of consciousness developed. "In a general atmosphere of questioning and heightened political activity, there grew a revitalized element among Mexican Americans which can rightfully call itself the Chicano movement." With those words, Van H. Garner described the beginning of a new era in the attempt to achieve the American dream.

In 1960 there were 4 million Mexicans legally living in the United States; that number has grown to approximately 10 million today (1977). The sheer increase in numbers, plus the development of several articulate leaders with the ability to use the media for publicity, has brought the Chicano to public attention. His visibility during the past fifteen years has been intensified to a degree unimagined before.

Among the numerous young Mexican leaders who emerged during the 1960s, Reis Lopez Tijerina, Rodolfo Gonzales, and

Cesar Chavez were three of the most important. Tijerina ("el Tigre") focused his attention on land reform. Since the Treaty of Guadelupe Hidalgo, Mexican Americans had been separated from much of the land guaranteed them by that treaty. Tijerina and his followers, in 1963, took over a portion of Kit Carson National Park in New Mexico and set up their own country, the Republic of San Juan del Rio de Chama. While their "invasion" was doomed to failure, it did capture headlines and dramatized the plight of the Chicano. Tijerina has since turned to La Raza Unida Party (the United Chicano Party).

"Corky" Gonzales, at one time contender for the World Featherweight boxing crown, and later a successful businessman in Denver, Colorado, returned to the barrio (ghetto) and organized La Crusada Paro la Justicia (Crusade for Justice) in 1965. This organization promoted a new sense of ethnic pride among Mexican Americans and led in 1969 to the first Chicano Liberation Conference. In 1970, during a Los Angeles march, Gonzales was arrested and convicted on a charge of carrying a loaded gun. He served twenty-eight of a forty-day jail sentence and then, like Tijerina before him, moved into La Raza Unida Party.

The most effective figure as a unifying symbol, and certainly the most lasting Chicano leader to emerge during this period, is Cesar Chavez. Chavez, who worked for the Community Service Organization from 1952 until the early 1960s, was originally hired to organize Mexican Americans in California. He resigned his CSO post in 1962 in protest over its clearly structured middle class value system and its refusal to become involved with migrant workers.

Between 1962 and 1965 Chavez began organizing farm workers, and in the latter year he and his newly organized union, the United Farm Workers Association, challenged California agribusiness with the famous Delano, California, grape strike (huelga). Utilizing boycott tactics reminiscent of the Montgomery bus boycott of ten years earlier, except for the national scope of the grape boycott, Chavez's union held out until the grape growers finally signed with the UFW in 1970. In the process the Chicano picked up numerous friends and supporters and genuine national sympathy. Robert Kennedy's support was invaluable in terms of national publicity, but possibly just as important was the support given by Walter

Reuther of the United Auto Workers and H.L. Mitchell. Mitchell, an old-line American socialist who had helped form the biracial Southern Tenant Farmers Union in the 1930s, offered tactical advice and claimed the UFW was "an extension of the old STFU."

After the 1970 victory, after five years of strikes and boycotts, the Chavez forces found the victory bittersweet. At the same time that the grape growers signed with the UFW, lettuce growers attacked the Chicano movement in another way: they invited in the Teamsters Union! At that stage confusion set in. Thousands of farm workers were saying, "we want a union of our own," while Teamster officials argued that "farm workers want to belong to the Teamsters Union," and some growers were still maintaining that "our workers don't want a union" at all.

Three years later, in 1973, when the agreement between the grape growers and the UFW expired, contracts went to the Teamsters. For two years there was an intense struggle between the Teamsters and the UFW with a good deal of violence, including the murder of three UFW members. With California's new governor Jerry Brown promoting action, in 1975 the California State Legislature passed a law which would allow workers to decide by vote which union would represent them. That was essentially the last Chicano victory, and the UFW still struggles just to stay even, or, as Pat Hoffman has put it: the UFW has "the job of holding justice ground" gained, it cannot be concerned with "gaining justice ground." In a perceptive statement relative to the future of the Chicano movement, Chavez said in an October 1977 interview: "Power is very elusive. It is here today and gone tomorrow."

Even the Chicano Studies programs begun in the early 1970s at all levels of education have begun to fade. The nation appears today to be less sensitive than it was five years ago with regard to injustices committed against the Chicano. In spite of the ever-increasing numbers, Chicanos are rarely found in any positions of political power. Unfortunately, even Cesar Chavez's image has been tarnished. He is currently under attack from within his own community for a fall, 1977, trip to the Philippines as the guest of repressive right-wing President Ferdinand Marco's military dictatorship. To quote Van H. Garner: "The mood of the mid-seventies is characterized by indecision, and it has engulfed the Chicano movement as well."

Any general evaluation of the present status of those struggling Americans discussed in this essay must of necessity be subjective. Contrary, perhaps, to John Steinbeck's assertion, these groups have worked out a definition of the American dream on their own terms. In each instance, in the beginning, the focus of their dreams has been on the material. The desire for economic progress, the quest for the material advantages of the majority around them, has motivated these dispossessed people. In all cases, however, even when economic security has not been obtained, each group has broadened its meaning of the dream to include another dimension: pride, culture, heritage, self-determination, and consciousness of self as an integral part of society. In the words of Ms. Ashley, blacks, Indians, women, and Chicanos have realized that oppression has "crippled and handicapped by poverty in spirit as well as in purse." While not denying that some progress has been made (each group has benefited from the numerous antidiscrimination measures passed by Congress during the past decade), these struggling Americans still await liberation.

SUGGESTED READINGS

The sources for an essay of this nature are primarily journalistic. Most important have been such contemporary journals as *Newsweek*, *Time*, *The New York Times Magazine*, *Christianity Today*, *Sojourners*, and *The Other Side*. The last two journals have recently devoted whole issues to the Chicano and Indian movements; and *Christianity Today* has conducted in-depth interviews with such movement people as Jesse Jackson, Eldridge Cleaver, Cesar Chavez, and Nancy Hardesty.

A short book, which includes material relevant to each of the groups discussed in this essay, is Norman Rosenberg, Emily Rosenberg, and James Moore, *In Our Times: America Since World War II* (1976). For the Indian movement, see Donald J. Berthong, "The American Indian: From Pacificism to Activism," *The Forum Series* (1973). More comprehensive is Wilcomb E. Washburn, *The Indian in America* (1975). Any study of the women's liberation movement should begin with Betty Friedan, *The Feminine Mystique* (1963). For a good historical analysis, see William Chafe, *The American Woman:*

Her Changing Social, Economic and Political Role, 1920-1970 (1972). Two collections of essays and primary sources pertinent to the American woman are Nancy L. Cott, (ed.), *Root of Bitterness* (1972), and Jean E. Friedman and William G. Shade, (eds.), *Our American Sisters* (1973). For Chicano Liberation see Van H. Garner, "Conflict and Resistance: The Chicano in the Twentieth Century," *Forums in History* (1974). Excellent, and very thorough, is Rudolfo Acuna, *Occupied America: The Chicano's Struggle Toward Liberation* (1972). For the historical background of the black struggle, John Hope Franklin, *From Slavery to Freedom* (1967), is standard. Helpful in sorting out works and evaluating them is John W. Blassingame, "The Afro-American: From Mythology to Reality," in *The Reinterpretation of American History* (1973). See also Floyd Barbour, (ed.), *The Black Power Revolt: A Collection of Essays* (1968), and Theodore Draper's *The Rediscovery of Black Nationalism* (1970).

Senator Joseph R. McCarthy and the counsel for the United States Army, Joseph Welch, at the Army-McCarthy hearings, Spring 1954. (United Press International)

CHAPTER ELEVEN

Hysteria in Twentieth Century America

FRANCIS THOMPSON

To find the roots of hysteria in American history it would be necessary to go back at least to the passage of the Alien and Sedition Acts in 1798 and the subsequent panic over a possible war with France. At various times since, the nation has been occupied by the fear of Irish Catholics, immigrants in general, and assorted others of every stripe and shade. As the nation entered the twentieth century, many native-born Americans were evidencing a special apprehension over the flood of new immigrants entering the country, and the movement to "close the gates" was daily growing more intense.

Nativism was not a new phenomenon in United States history, having surfaced in the 1850s with the outbursts against Irish Catholics. After a period of quiescence, the nativists regrouped in the 1880s for a major effort to restrict or exclude Eastern Europeans and Asians. In 1882, Congress passed legislation that provided for a ten-year exclusion on immigration from China. The law was extended several times and finally made permanent in 1902. The final Act also denied Chinese already in the country the right to become naturalized citizens. Although few Japanese citizens migrated to the United States, a large number of citizens on the West Coast were anxious to extend exclusionist laws to that Asian nationality.

In 1906, the school board of the city of San Francisco, in a precipitous action, totally segregated Japanese, Chinese, and

Korean children in the public schools of that city. The Japanese government filed an immediate and strongly worded protest. President Theodore Roosevelt, fearing a complete rupture of United States relations with Japan, pressured the San Francisco board of education to rescind the segregation order. Through a series of notes over the next two years, Roosevelt secured the so-called "Gentlemen's Agreement" between the United States and Japan in which the latter agreed to issue no more passports to the mainland United States. The state of California followed with a number of laws restricting Japanese immigration from Hawaii, and in 1913 secured passage of legislation to prohibit Japanese ownership of land in California. Doubtless the nativist groups breathed a collective sigh of relief after their successful campaign to close the door to the "yellow peril"; little, however, had been done to restrict entrance of the less desirable Europeans.

In the same year as the Chinese Exclusion Act, 1882, Congress introduced the first real restriction on European immigration by imposing a fifty cents head tax on each immigrant, to be paid by the steamship company that provided the transportation. By 1904, the head tax had been increased to four dollars. Such meager restrictions did not satisfy the diehard nativists, especially those members of the Immigration Restriction League, founded in 1894 by a group of New England intellectuals and the spearhead for restriction outside Congress for the next twenty-six years. In part a response to the pressures exerted by the League, Senator Henry Cabot Lodge of Massachusetts, in 1896, proposed a literacy test for all new immigrants. Lodge made no attempt to conceal what group of aliens the test was designed to omit when he declared, in a speech before Congress, that it would "bear most heavily upon the Italians, Russians, Poles, Hungarians, Greeks, and Asiatics. . . . " The Congress passed legislation providing for such a literacy test but it was successfully vetoed by President Grover Cleveland. A similar bill was vetoed in 1913 by President William Howard Taft and it was also sustained. Still a third literacy test bill was passed in 1915, but again vetoed with success by then President Woodrow Wilson. The restrictionists were a determined and unrelenting lot and a fourth bill finally became law over Wilson's second veto in 1917. Although the imposition of such a literacy test represented the first significant restriction of Europeans, the major legislation to restrict immigration would be passed in the midst of nativist panic that followed World War I.

An important aspect of nativism in the early twentieth century was the completely false notion held by many Americans that aliens as a rule tended to become radicals. Though it was true that immigrants constituted a large portion of the membership of most radical groups in this country, the socialists, anarchists, and others, the total membership of such organizations never amounted to more than a handful. The overwhelming majority of immigrants were politically conservative, as evidenced by their refusal to support even the most moderate reform movements.

There was also a significant number of United States citizens who felt that the labor movement was more than a little tinged by foreign radicalism. This, too, was a faulty assumption. Rank and file labor for the most part supported the conservative directives of labor leaders such as Samuel Gompers. This was clearly illustrated when a number of radicals, including socialists Eugene V. Debs and Daniel DeLeon, met in Chicago in 1905 to organize the International Workers of the World. The Wobblies, as they were generally known, disavowed the conservative tendencies of Gompers and the AFL; their goal was to mobilize all workers into one big union, paralyze the capitalist system with massive strikes, then establish an economy run entirely by the workers. Such radical ideas would eventually drive most of the socialists from the ranks of the IWW.

By 1908, William "Big Bill" Haywood, a wild, revolutionary, one-eyed miner from Montana, had become the undisputed leader of the Wobblies. Under his direction, the organization would attract its strongest support from transient workers in the West, lumberjacks, those who followed the wheat harvests, and casual workers on the West Coast. Many Americans viewed the IWW's appeal as directed less at workers than to those in the society who were not fully supportive of the Protestant work ethic. As noted in the Los Angeles *Times*: "A vast number of IWW's are non-producers. IWW stands for I won't work, and I want whisky. . . . "

Despite their revolutionary zeal, which was refreshing in a sense, the membership of the IWW never exceeded more than 60,000, nor did they at any time present a serious threat to the more established unions. Indeed, the inflammatory rhetoric of the IWW so frightened both the business community and the general public, that it made the conservative policies of the AFL even more acceptable. In the end, the Wobblies, along with other radical groups, would be swallowed up in the repression of a war that touched off a tidal wave of fear and hysteria that would not subside for many decades.

President Woodrow Wilson's warning that once this nation went to war, it would forget the meaning of tolerance proved sadly prophetic. The Committee on Public Information, headed by journalist George Creel, was established to mobilize the American mind for the crusade against the infamous and barbaric German Hun. The Creel Committee's efforts represented a classic case of "over-kill" which initiated a period of organized hysteria that would extend far beyond the Armistice of 1918. Americans grew to hate not only the Kaiser but German Americans as well, many of whom had lived in this country for several generations. Congress responded to the fear in 1917 by passing the Espionage Act which provided for a $10,000 fine or twenty years imprisonment for anyone

> Whoever, when the United States is at war . . . shall wilfully utter, print, write, or publish any disloyal, profane, scurrilous, or abusive language about the form of government of the United States, or the Constitution of the United States, or the military or naval forces of the United States, or the flag . . . or the uniform of the Army or Navy of the United States, or any language intended to bring the form of government . . . or the Constitution . . . of the United States into contempt, scorn, . . . or disrepute. . . .
>
> or
>
> shall wilfully cause . . . or incite . . . insubordination, disloyalty, mutiny, or refusal of duty, in the military or naval forces of the United States, or shall wilfully obstruct . . . the recruiting or enlistment service of the United States. . . .

The legislation was used less against potential subversion than to eliminate, with its catch-all provisions, any criticism of the war. The Sedition Act of 1918 was less subtle. It was used from the first to promote conformity.

The extreme hysteria and intolerance that so characterized the period of World War I continued, indeed intensified, after the war ended. Germany was defeated but the Communist menace precipitated a new era of hysteria. The Bolshevik Revolution in Russia aroused anxieties in the United States that have not yet abated. Most of the subsurface fears that Americans had felt for decades suddenly became intertwined with communism, i.e. Communists want to integrate the races, Communists precipitate labor violence, immigrants tend to become Communists. In short, any examination of American hysteria since World War I must seriously consider the fact that later periods of intense fear in the United States are to a large degree rooted in a deep-seated preoccupation with red communism.

This fact was clearly illustrated in the period of labor unrest that immediately followed World War I. The large number of strikes that swept the country in 1919 greatly alarmed the business community. The Bolsheviks, many concluded, were out to overthrow American capitalism. Whether such conclusions were real or concocted, the American businessman succeeded in transferring his fear of Bolshevism to the public in general and state legislatures in particular. Thirty-five of the forty-eight states had passed restrictive labor legislation by 1920.

On the national level, the red scare was led by Attorney General A. Mitchell Palmer and his close confidants in the Department of Justice. One of the more prominent among the latter was J. Edgar Hoover, future head of the Federal Bureau of Investigation. In the early months of 1920, Palmer initiated a number of hunts that yielded several thousand aliens, many of whom were eventually deported. May Day 1920 passed without incident (Hoover had predicted massive demonstrations) and the nation began to regain some measure of its sanity.

The post-World War I witch hunt introduced a new dimension of intolerance in the United States — the emergence of the demagogues and special interest groups who sought to exploit the nation's paranoia over the devil communism. It was a short but unhappy road that connected the 1920 red scare, led by an Attorney General, and the period of red hysteria that followed World War II; hysteria that was so skillfully manipulated by a number of people, one of whom, Richard M. Nixon, would ride the crusade all the way to the White House.

Although the intensity of the 1919-1920 scare had subsided by the last months of 1920, the xenophobia aroused by Palmer and his associates continued throughout the twenties. One manifestation of such fear was the dramatic growth of the Ku

Klux Klan which broadened its attack to cover Catholics, Jews, and anyone else who voiced ideas that differed from those espoused by the exalted leaders of the "invisible empire." The Klan drew much of its strength from rural elements opposed to modernity in American life. Still, the Ku Klux Klan was symptomatic of an intolerant decade and the activities of that organization helped create the atmosphere that moved the Congress to pass a series of restrictive immigration laws — to establish quotas that would restrict or deny entrance to the "less desirable" aliens.

The plight of the alien in such a frightened and intolerant time can be no better illustrated than in the arrest, trial, and subsequent executions of Nicola Sacco and Bartolomeo Vanzetti for a murder committed during a labor disturbance near Boston, Massachusetts, in 1920. Guilt or innocence notwithstanding, historical evidence clearly indicates that the two men did not receive a fair trial — that they were the victims of an unreasoning fear of anything foreign. Vanzetti's statement during the trial had the ring of truth. "I am suffering because I am a radical and indeed I am a radical; I have suffered because I was an Italian, and indeed I am an Italian. . . . "

Sacco and Vanzetti, after the failure of many efforts to spare their lives, were executed in 1927. The following year, the nation underwent another outburst of intolerance in the disgraceful anti-Catholic campaign waged against Al Smith, the Democratic nominee for President. Although the evidence suggests that Republican Herbert Hoover would probably have won in any case, the abusive attacks against Smith's religion was yet another symptom of the bigotry and fear that was so much a part of the Roaring Twenties.

The election of Herbert Hoover, a decent man whatever his failings, offered some hope that the nation might regain its sanity which had been collectively lost since the declaration of war in 1917. Before Hoover had time to adjust himself to his new position, however, the stock market crash ushered in the age of the Great Depression. For millions of Americans, the imagined fears of the twenties were soon replaced by the more realistic threat of economic collapse.

The deepening economic crisis served to escalate fears of Communist infiltration and prompted a number of Congressional investigations. One of the first was chaired by conservative Republican Representative Hamilton Fish from New York. The Fish Committee, after six months of hearings in 1930, concluded that the Communist party in the United States was revolutionary, that it owed allegiance to the Communist International, and that its further activities should be outlawed in the United States. No legislative action was taken on the Fish Committee report.

Additional hearings were conducted in 1934-1935 by a select committee headed jointly by Representatives John McCormick of Massachusetts and Samuel Dickstein of New York. Although the McCormick-Dickstein Committee devoted most of its time to Fascist activity, the Communist problem was not overlooked. Earl Browder, Executive Secretary of the Central Committee of the Communist Party in the United States, estimated Communist party membership at 24,000 in 1934, with many thousands of other supporters who sympathized with the party's goals. The Congress later acted on two of the proposals made by the McCormick-Dickstein Committee, the most important being a statute that required the registration of foreign agents.

In April 1937, Representative Dickstein proposed the establishment of a permanent committee for the principal purpose of investigating Nazi activities; his subsequent resolution to that effect was denied. The reason most often stated for the refusal was that such a committee might act as a stimulant to anti-Semitism. The outlook changed so dramatically in the next year, with the Fascist takeover in Czechoslovakia, that a similar proposal passed under the authorship of Texas Representative Martin Dies who became the first chairman of the temporary House Committee on Un-American Activities; it would not become a permanent committee of Congress until 1945. The activities of such a group, Harry Truman later concluded, set the precedent "which has plagued the Congress ever since."

It had been assumed that a committee on "un-American" activities would investigate the scope and range of any group or organization that might fall into that category. Indeed, one of the strongest initial supporters for the establishment of such an investigative group was the NAACP which mistakenly thought that the Ku Klux Klan would come under close scrutiny. It soon became apparent, however, that the chairman's interest was more restricted. From the outset, the House Committee concentrated on the menace of communism. The demagogues and super patriots were prepared to lead the nation on a witch hunt from which it has yet to fully recover.

The red scare was delayed by the United States' entrance into World War II and our subsequent alliance with Soviet Russia. Although the country appeared solidly united behind the war effort, the 1941-1945 period was not without its moments of intolerance. The most glaring example was the incarceration of Japanese Americans living on the West Coast. Thousands of United States citizens of Japanese ancestry were suddenly and without any reasonable justification, deprived of their property and sent to internment camps scattered throughout the Southwest. The move represented a flagrant violation of both constitutional and human rights. But, with this one horrible exception, the World War II period was remarkably free of the wild hysteria that so characterized our participation in World War I.

The euphoria that followed the defeat of Germany and Japan was of short duration, due in a large measure to the almost immediate deterioration in relations between the United States and the USSR. The onslaught of the Cold War, and the new and frightening threat of atomic disaster, combined to awaken the nation anew to the "red menace." The mounting hysteria was encouraged by many in positions of influence who collectively insisted that Communist agents had so successfully infiltrated the government service in the 1930s and 1940s that they had significantly influenced the formulation of American foreign and domestic policy.

Although there was certainly infiltration, particularly in the Department of Agriculture, the available evidence suggests that internal communism never posed the danger that some would have had the nation believe. The red hunters glibly ignored such evidence, however, and proceeded on their search for Communists at every stump and crossroads. Reluctantly, Harry Truman finally yielded to the pressure and in March 1947 issued Executive Order 9835 creating a loyalty program that provided for at least a cursory examination of the files of every individual employed by the federal government. Such a widespread investigation wasted much time, injured the reputations of many innocent people, and, in the end, yielded few real subversives. However, many individuals in and out of Congress insisted that the president's program did not go far enough — that Communists were still operating with impunity. As a result, Congress intensified its investigations.

Few were immune to the surveillance of the red hunters. In March 1947, the House Committee on Un-American Activities launched a full-scale investigation of supposed Communist influence in the film industry. Outside Congress, three ex-FBI agents published several pamphlets, the most damaging entitled *Red Channels*, that proposed to reveal the random Communist connections of individuals in a number of professional fields; teachers, textbooks, and curriculum also received close attention. Such exposés resulted in the eventual blacklisting of hundreds of individuals, many of whom would never work again in their chosen fields.

The hysteria continued to build when suddenly, in February 1950, the junior Senator from Wisconsin, Joseph R. McCarthy, stepped from virtual obscurity to take command of the anti-Communist crusade. Speaking before a group of Republican ladies at a Lincoln birthday celebration in Wheeling, West Virginia, McCarthy announced that he had secured a list of 205 (or was it 81, or 57? — he could never remember the exact number he used) individuals who were card-carrying Communists and working in the Department of State. The speech launched McCarthy's four-year campaign of smear and innuendo.

Richard Rovere, author of a critical biography, declared that Senator McCarthy "was in many ways the most gifted demagogue ever bred on these shores. No bolder seditionist ever moved among us, nor any politician with a surer, swifter access to the dark places of the American mind." McCarthy was assuredly a master of the "big lie," and he followed with perfection the advice of a Senate colleague who exhorted him to keep up the accusations until he found one that really fit. In the early stages of the Senate subcommittee's investigation of McCarthy's allegations, the Senator suddenly named Professor Owen Lattimore, then on special assignment from the United Nations to Afghanistan, as the " 'top Soviet espionage agent' in the State Department." McCarthy informed the committee that he would rest his entire case on that one charge:

> I am telling you that this is the one case in which I think we can easily have a determination by this committee as to whether or not my charges are well founded or not.

After a thorough examination of Lattimore's loyalty files, the committee chairman, Millard Tydings, announced that nothing had been found to indicate that the professor was or ever had been disloyal to the United States. McCarthy had obviously missed the mark but it did not deter him in the least. He simply dismissed the whole investigation as a whitewash and was quickly off in another direction. As was his custom, the Senator always managed to stay several charges ahead of his opponents.

Through it all, the majority in Congress appeared cowed and the administration, mired in a desperate struggle against Communist forces in Korea, found itself continually on the defensive against McCarthy's numerous attacks. The overall effect produced an unhealthy state of conformity which made difficult, if not impossible, any sane, sensible discussions of the serious problems of the time.

Joe McCarthy remained a dominant figure on the American political scene until 1954 when he finally overextended himself with his investigation of the army. Thirty-five days of televised hearings exposed graphically the Senator's shortcomings to the American viewing public. A short time after the hearings concluded, McCarthy was "reprimanded" by his own Senate colleagues, many of whom had been most reluctant to speak out against him before that time. From that point, he faded rapidly from the public view. In 1957, Joseph R. McCarthy died in virtual obscurity.

Perhaps the people had grown weary of Joe McCarthy, or perhaps the fear had simply run its course. A very plausible explanation, at least in part, for the demise of McCarthy is that he was from the first a highly effective political tool whose job it was to harry the Democrats from office by identifying that party with Communist infiltration. Dean Acheson, in his *Present at the Creation*, referred to the Wisconsin Senator as "essentially a lazy, small-town bully, without sustaining purpose, who on his own would soon have petered out." He did, in fact, "peter out" rather quickly after the Republicans returned to power in 1953.

Whatever the case, the intensity of the red scare was on the wane by the mid-1950s. Communism continued to be the number one menace in the minds of many, and conformity remained the order of the day, but with the fall of "tailgunner Joe," the anti-red crusade had lost its leading exponent. Unfortunately, the effects of the red scare extended far beyond the life of its most devoted disciple.

The era of McCarthyism, the name applied to the entire period of red hysteria, dominated the attention of the government, indeed the nation, for almost ten years from the conclusion of World War II. At that critical period in the nation's history, a time when public officials should have been engaged in meaningful debate on ways and means to cope with the problems of a society in flux, the government found itself engaged in a wasteful, destructive, and unnecessary witch hunt. In addition, the random attacks on government employees made it virtually impossible to develop any sort of rational, long-range foreign policy, especially with regard to the Far East. The series of misguided decisions that eventually led the United States into the Vietnam disaster can be traced in a large part to the stultifying effect of McCarthyism.

Finally, there is no accurate way to measure the impact of the McCarthy era on the people involved — those affected either directly or indirectly. Of the literally thousands charged at one time or another, there were undoubtedly a few whose loyalty may well have been suspect. The government certainly has a duty as well as a right to protect itself from such persons. There is no right, however, indeed no place in a free society, for character assassination — for making reckless charges based on little more than rumor, gossip, or hearsay. In the final analysis, there was a string of damaged or ruined reputations, and the biggest loser was the nation as a whole.

To many young Americans, McCarthyism was a passing phenomenon of the late 1940s and 1950s. Such a dastardly thing, some may say, could never happen again. It unhappily might if the people do not make an effort to understand and recognize the American propensity for occasional paranoia. The same anxieties that allowed millions to listen and believe the nativists outcrys also supported A. Mitchell Palmer, the Ku Klux Klan, and Joe McCarthy.

During times of turbulence and uncertainty, there are always that number, a minority hopefully, but dangerous nevertheless, who have demonstrated a certain willingness to surrender traditional freedoms in search of some illusive tranquility. Doubtless there are many among that hysterical fringe that even yet attempt to justify the recent misdoings of the Nixon administration as "necessary evils," required to protect the nation from some imagined danger. Such individuals should take heed of the words of Andrew Jackson who declared, quite properly, that "there are no necessary evils in a free government."

Through it all, the outbursts of hate, intolerance, bigotry, and fear, the nation has always managed to emerge intact, albeit bruised. Such endurance is a tribute to our free institutions. But can we be assured that it will always be so? The best that can be hoped for is that people can and will make reasonable, intelligent distinctions between those in positions of trust and influence who appeal to the fears and anxieties in the national character, and the others who call forth the best of human instincts — and follow the latter. It may sound idealistic — even utopian — but it is our best hope to avoid future periods of distasteful and dangerous national hysteria.

SUGGESTED READINGS

On the problems of the immigrant in American society, Oscar Handlin, *The Uprooted* is still one of the best, most sensitive accounts. John Higham, *Strangers in the Land: Patterns of American Nativism, 1860-1925* gives a good account of the nativist mentality. For a look at the IWW, see Melvyn Dubofsky, *We Shall Be All: A History of the International Workers of the World.* For labor's problems after World War I, consult David Bordy, *Labor in Crisis, 1919.* James R. Monck and Cedric Larson, *Words That Won the War: The Story of the Committee on Public Information* is a good account of wartime propaganda. Also valuable is William Preston, Jr., *Aliens and Dissension: Federal Suppression of Radicals, 1903-1933.* For a general account of the twenties see William E. Leuchtenburg, *The Perils of Prosperity, 1914-1932.* The best overall study of the postwar hysteria is Robert Murray, *Red Scare: A Study in National Hysteria.* On the Ku Klux Klan, see David M. Chalmers, *Hooded Americanism: The First Century of the Ku Klux Klan.* G. Louis Joughlin and Edward F. Morgan, *The Legacy of Sacco and Vanzetti* provide valuable insight on the famous Sacco-Vanzetti trial. A good general account of the pre-World War II fear of communism is Earl Latham, *The Communist Controversy in Washington: From the New Deal to McCarthy.* On the most serious infringements of civil liberties in World War II see Dillon S. Meyer, *Uprooted Americans: The Japanese Americans and the War Relocation Authority During World War II.* On the problems of postwar loyalty, Richard M. Freeland, *The Truman Doctrine and the Origins of McCarthyism* places much of the blame for the hysteria on Truman. Alan Harper, *The Politics of Loyalty: The White House and the Communist Issue* is a more balanced account. In addition to the authors already cited on McCarthy, one of the best accounts is Robert Griffith, *The Politics of Fear: Joseph R. McCarthy and The Senate.* On the army-McCarthy hearings, see Michael Straight, *Trial by Television.* An excellent examination of the whole issue of free speech is found in Zechariah Chafee, *Free Speech in The United States.* Stefan Kamfer, *A Journal of The Plague Years* gives a lucid and interesting account of the Hollywood hearings and the practice of blacklisting in the 1950s.

FORUM PRESS